Praise for *Goal-Free Living*

"Stephen Shapiro has written a smart, practical, and inspiring guide to leading a life of purpose and meaning. If you have only one goal this year, let it be this: read *Goal-Free Living*!"

> —Daniel H. Pink, Author of *A Whole New Mind*
> and *Free Agent Nation*

"Stephen Shapiro's *Goal-Free Living* isn't a call for laziness, passivity, or risk mongering. Instead, his approach will help readers achieve the best kind of happenstance; taking a stance to make things happen."

> —Heath Row, Contributing Editor and
> Community Director, *Fast Company* Magazine

"Stephen Shapiro shows how individuals can find more joy in life while still making important contributions to society and the people around them. The insights in *Goal-Free Living* will be valuable to anyone who feels consumed or constrained by their own goals. I have a sense reading this book may turn out to be one of the most important things I've done in a long time."

> —Doug Busch, Vice President and Chief Technology
> Officer, Digital Health Group, Intel Corporation

"In this insightful, charming book Stephen Shapiro guides you to reframe the way you think about goals. This is an engaging, creative approach to discovering inner wisdom and personal fulfillment."

> —Michael J. Gelb, Author of *How to Think Like*
> *Leonardo Da Vinci* and *Discover Your Genius*

"Reading *Goal-Free Living* is like jettisoning a hundred-pound pack. Suddenly, you're racing much faster and enjoying the breeze."

> —Alan Weiss, Ph.D., Author of
> *Million Dollar Consulting*

"Steve is brilliantly insightful. He knows (and this book proves) that it is the pursuit of what you love, not the achievement of your goals, that will give you a joyful and passionate life."

—Marcia Wieder, America's Dream Coach®,
Author of *Making Your Dreams Come True*

"Stephen Shapiro powerfully shows that true success is not determined by the goals we achieve, but rather by the life we live. *Goal-Free Living* is YOUR guide for having the life you want NOW!"

—Marshall Goldsmith, Author (or co-editor) of
19 books, including *The Leader of the Future*
(recognized in the *Wall Street Journal* as
one of the top 10 executive educators)

"Despite the paradoxical title, the book's thesis and purpose are straightforward. Although creativity cannot be forced, one must be prepared for it. Shapiro shows how being goal-free can be a catalyst for personal growth, achievement, and satisfaction."

—Al Gini, Professor of Philosophy at Loyola University
Chicago, Author of *The Importance of Being Lazy*
and *My Job My Self*

"If you've ever imagined living a completely different life, this book will inspire you to take a step toward a more exciting future. Trying just one of the eight secrets will result in a dramatic and positive shift in your perspective."

—Alan Price, Author of *Ready to Lead*

Goal-Free Living

Goal-Free Living

How to Have the Life You Want NOW!

STEPHEN M. SHAPIRO

WILEY

JOHN WILEY & SONS, INC.

Published by John Wiley & Sons, Inc., Hoboken, New Jersey.
Published simultaneously in Canada.

For general information on our other products and services or for technical support, please contact our Customer Care Department within the United States at (800) 762-2974, outside the United States at (317) 572-3993 or fax (317) 572-4002.

Wiley also publishes its books in a variety of electronic formats. Some content that appears in print may not be available in electronic books. For more information about Wiley products, visit our web site at www.wiley.com.

Library of Congress Cataloging-in-Publication Data:

Shapiro, Stephen, 1964–
    Goal-free living : how to have the life you want now! / Stephen Shapiro.
      p. cm.
    ISBN-13: 978-0-471-77280-4 (cloth)
    ISBN-10: 0-471-77280-1 (cloth)
    1. Lifestyles.   2. Quality of life.   3. Life skills.   I. Title.
HQ2042.S53   2006
646.7—dc22
                                          2005021405

Printed in the United States of America.

10 9 8 7 6 5 4 3 2 1

DID YOU KNOW THAT...

- 41 percent of Americans say that achieving their goals has not made them happier and has only left them disillusioned? That is over 100 million people.

- 33 percent of Americans have lost sleep over their goals? That's one out of every three Americans.

- Nearly one out of five Americans (18 percent) have wrecked a friendship, marriage, or relationship because of a goal they were trying to achieve? These people are three times as likely to be unhappy as people who were not such extreme goalaholics.

- 27 percent of Americans—one in four—say that achieving their financial goals has not made them happier? Even some of the wealthiest individuals say this.

- 29 percent of Americans say they think they might have chosen the wrong goals in life?

- One out of seven, 13 percent of this country, has been so obsessed with achieving a goal that at one point in their lives they broke the law or did something unethical? And those are only the ones who admit it.

- 36 percent of Americans say that the more goals they set for themselves, the more stressed out they become, while 52 percent say that one of their goals is to reduce the amount of stress in their lives? This is incredibly ironic.

- Only 8 percent of Americans always achieve their New Year's resolutions? 92 percent fail!

- 31 percent of Americans say that they are currently goal-free? Do they know something that you don't?

Our achievement-oriented society has hijacked our happiness. Fight back. Now is the time to take control and free yourself from the stranglehold of goals that grips so many people.

Based on a random telephone survey conducted by Goalfree.com, with the assistance of Opinion Research Corporation of Princeton, New Jersey. The survey of 1,012 individuals has a margin of error of 3 percent and was conducted during the period August 5 to August 8, 2005.

CONTENTS

ACKNOWLEDGMENTS

A book about extraordinary living could not exist without the contributions of a large number of extraordinary people. I am honored to have met and worked with so many such individuals over the past few years on this effort.

Goal-Free Living was born out of my travels during the summer of 2003 when I met and interviewed 150 passionate individuals. The chronicles of their lives provide the richness and texture of this book. Thank you for sharing your most personal stories with a complete stranger.

Given that I applied a goal-free approach to my writing, it is not surprising that the earliest versions of the manuscript were a bit disorganized. It is for that reason that I am truly indebted to the hard work of Ela Aktay Booty, who worked tirelessly to fine-tune the manuscript with the precision of a surgeon. Special thanks also to Michael Johnson, who was involved from a strategic perspective from the very beginning.

I am grateful for the many reviewers who provided inspiration, content, and brutally honest feedback—Ron Anderson, Susan Baird, Jason Bates, Jennifer Buchholz, Michael Herman, Brad Kolar, David Macintosh, Don Mitchell, Georgiana Philips, Lisa Rosenthal, Margarita Rozenfeld, Steve Stanton, Doug Stevenson, Don Ulibarri, and Shannon Vargo.

Many thanks to all of the great people at John Wiley &

Sons, Inc., in particular Matt Holt. Without Matt's support of this countercultural concept, this book might never have seen the light of day.

It has been an honor to be working with one of the best literary agents, Ned Levitt. His balance of steadfast support with probing challenge helped nurture this book's development.

I am blessed to have an incredible and loving family. My sister, Deborah, has been a source of inspiration. Our almost daily phone conversations and e-mail exchanges provided an endless supply of content, were an invaluable sounding board, and kept me sane. Gary, thank you for "lending" her to me.

Finally, words cannot express my gratitude for the contribution my parents have made. Thank you for providing the foundation that enabled my incredible and miraculous life.

PROLOGUE:
CONFESSIONS
OF A GOALAHOLIC

*M*y story starts June 1986 in Ithaca, New York. It was a time of possibility and new beginnings. I had graduated from Cornell University with a degree in Industrial Engineering and started a career with one of the top consulting firms in the world. At that time I was also dating a great woman, Beth Anne. On August 31st of the same year we were married at a small bed-and-breakfast in Massachusetts. Passion ignited my marriage; goals would kill it.

Here I was in a new marriage and a new job. My career was starting to take off. My first major consulting project was in New York City, developing a computer system using new and unproven technology. As expected, this project required long hours. Beth Anne and I lived in Connecticut, and the three-hour round trip commute to Brooklyn became unbearable. To reduce the travel time, the company put me up in an apartment with another employee in New York City. This meant that I saw Beth Anne only on weekends and sometimes not even then. Often I worked from 9 A.M. until 2 A.M. This routine continued for over a year. I became myopically focused on solving our numerous technical problems rather than the relationship problems looming right in front of me. My career clearly became the focus of my affections. In fact, success in consulting became my primary objective. Becoming a partner in this consulting firm materialized as a clear goal for me, even though that would be more than 10 years off in the horizon.

As one would expect, when working 80+ hours a week for extended periods of time, a new relationship is difficult to nurture. Beth Anne (rightly so) felt neglected. The intensity of my work was rapidly destroying our marriage. I was not spending time with her, and when we were together I was too tired. My goals were getting the best of me.

After several years, Beth Anne decided we should go our separate ways. She was right. We had grown so far apart that splitting up was the only option. This proved to be a very painful time for me. Only after our separation did I realize that my marriage mattered more than my job. But it was too late. I went into a funk and started to reevaluate my priorities.

I'm not sure if my goals drove me to work the crazy hours I did or if I used my goals as an excuse to avoid issues in my personal life. In any case, I got so wrapped up with work and success that I forgot to have a life. Is this what I really wanted? I began to think that maybe having a successful career was not the most important thing in my life. My immediate thought was to leave the consulting world altogether and pursue something I really loved—whatever that might be. Instead I decided to try a less radical route. I began doing more of the things that I enjoyed, such as playing my saxophone in local bands, while keeping my day job. All the while, work and chasing the goal of becoming a partner remained my top priorities.

I was whisked off to a project with a major corporation that needed to cut headcount to meet shareholder expectations. As usual, I was working long hours in a soulless, sterile corporate environment. The work that I was doing on this project would result in 10,000 people losing their jobs. A number that big was so impersonal that it was difficult to comprehend. I did not realize the impact our efforts would make on the lives of so many individuals. That is, until one day I saw a news program featuring a story about my client and three executives who had recently been let go. One was mowing lawns in order to make ends meet. He spent most of the interview crying. The second person was spending about 15 hours a day networking as he looked for another job. Although he had been unemployed for over a year, his story was the most upbeat of the three. The third person had committed suicide. The impact of just three layoffs became clear to me. The impact of 10,000 was unconscionable.

Once again, thoughts of leaving consulting rattled through my brain. Despite this existential crisis, I wasn't ready to leave the safety net of my successful career. In an effort to balance both financial security and personal satisfaction, the next day at work, I decided to take a two-month leave of absence. I could not continue to do work that would have such a negative impact on the lives of so many people.

During my time off, I took personal development classes, read books on Eastern philosophies, and spent days at the beach writing in a journal and thinking about what I should do. After eight weeks of introspection I came to a conclusion. I wanted a career that would inspire me. I wanted something that was aligned with my personal values, and I did not want to be responsible for so many lost jobs. Achieving my goals at the expense of my soul was not worth it.

I started thinking about growth rather than downsizing. Innovation and creativity rather than efficiency. I decided that within five years I wanted to be a leader in innovation, someone who could make a positive impact in the business world. I modeled my definition of success after a number of luminaries who spent their time giving keynote speeches, doing research, writing books, conducting training classes, traveling, and making a huge and visible impact in the world. That's what I wanted.

On the advice of friends and colleagues (and against my will), I pulled together a plan to achieve this goal. My handwritten plan was several pages long and detailed what I would be doing next week, next month, next year, and so on until five years had passed and my goal was achieved. Should I have chosen to follow this plan, I would have to work exceptionally hard, do work that did not interest me, and take lots of uninspiring classes. Basically I would need to dedicate my life to this goal for the next five years.

Soon afterwards, I had an interesting conversation with a friend, someone who clearly knew me better than I knew myself. She said, "I've noticed that people are asking you to design your future." She suggested, "Do not let them. In my eyes, you are like a frog. You should sun yourself on a lily pad until you get bored. Then, when the time is right, you should jump to a new lily pad and hang out there for a while. Continue this over and over, moving in whatever direction feels right." Her words resonated with me. Based on this insight, I decided to rip up my five-year plan. From that moment, the concept of being goal-free began to emerge in my mind. Today, I see that I can hop from experience to experience. Although each leap may build on the past, there are no specific goals or plans. Rather than forcing life down a particular path, I allow it to unfold before my eyes on many paths. My stays on each lily pad are not passive. Each lily pad hop brings me to a new set of active experiences where life is lived fully and passionately.

Even though I had already ripped up my plans for becoming a leader in the innovation space, I still had this as an aspiration — not as a goal but rather as an intention that subconsciously shifted my thoughts, feelings, and actions. Instead of taking the path that my now torn-up plan had so carefully charted, I decided to go down a different path. An unconventional path.

After several smaller hops, I took my first major leap off the lily pad and moved to London, still working in management consulting. I rented a small furnished one-bedroom apartment with a month-to-month lease. Living and working in England was an educational and enriching experience. While there, I chose projects of interest rather than those that would help my career. Flash ahead two years later — and five years after the declaration of my aspiration — when my book *24/7 Innovation* hit the bookstores. It was at that time that I decided to hop onto another lily pad.

I ditched my six-figure consulting job, moved out of my apartment, gave away most of my belongings, and began traveling the world. I created a business in which I would give speeches, conduct research, write books and articles, conduct training classes, and make an impact in the business world, much like the aspiration I had envisioned many years before. Although in my first year I took a 90 percent pay cut, I truly love my life. Money, status, and traditional success are no longer motivators. I now use a different measure of success, one built on contribution given rather than on monetary rewards received. In spite of this detachment from money, the business is thriving and evolving. This book represents another lily pad hop for me. I have no idea what the future holds. All I know is that I wake up every day energized, excited, and looking forward to seeing how things unfold.

Looking back, I realize that for a number of years I was a

goalaholic. My story is typical of many. Goals made me success-ful. Unfortunately, they provided little passion or satisfaction along the way. I didn't recognize this at the time. It was easy to get caught up in society's definition of success: money, status, and achievement. This is what we are all told is the best way to live. This book is about a new way to look at your life.

Yes, I still have a Type-A personality but I am a Goal-Free Type-A individual. I am committed to following my passion and playing hard in everything I do. It never feels like work. In fol-lowing my passion I often end up taking a different path than I originally imagined. Yet I still manage to be successful. I am proud to say that I have been goal-free for 10 years. My life has never been better.

The Genesis of This Book

I had found a formula that worked for me. I found it by luck and persistence. Now I needed to know how everyone could have a passion-filled life. I wanted to uncover an approach that could be replicated by anyone. To discover this, I took to the road during the summer of 2003 in search of ordinary people with extraordi-nary lives. During my travels and interviews, I learned the secret of this kind of achievement. It may surprise you, as it did me. It isn't about goals or about ambition. Instead, the secret is to treat your life like an unplanned and unpredictable trip down a scenic, winding country road. You are guided by your internal compass and you learn to follow your passions, even if they seem to be a detour. Every day is an adventure, with life unfolding before your eyes. You avoid setting large life goals so that you are free to focus on the present. You recognize that "success" without satisfaction is failure. Extraordinary living is understanding that simple satisfaction is personal success.

Over the course of 90 days, I drove 12,000 miles and interviewed 150 extraordinary people, many of whom are highlighted in this book. Using conventional logic, you may think that such an expedition would require detailed planning and incredible coordination. Not so. Instead, I set out without specific plans and allowed the trip to unfold naturally. In fact, it was only a week prior to the trip that I even started looking for people to interview. To get the word out, I distributed a press release, sent e-mails to people I knew, placed ads on Google and on my web site, contacted local media, and connected with the *Fast Company* magazine reader's network. This was all the planning I needed to get started.

On June 5, 2003, I left Boston in my Toyota Solara with only the first few days planned. As I drove south and made connections with new people, my plans evolved and changed. I made hotel reservations only on the day of my arrival in each city to maximize flexibility. I met people in their offices, in their living rooms, at Starbucks, in nursing homes, on the beach, or anywhere that we could best connect. Most interviews lasted two hours but some ran much longer. In total I amassed more than 150 audio tapes with hundreds of hours of conversation.

On my web site I kept readers up to date with my travels by charting where I had been and where I might be going. In addition, as I met people, I would post their pictures and a brief biography on my web site. Although I did not have a single interview lined up a week before my travels, I managed to conduct interviews every day of the trip. Some people I met had responded to ads and press releases—I received more than 500 e-mails from people who were interested in being interviewed. Others I contacted directly based on recommendations of friends and colleagues. Some of the most interesting individuals I discovered by chance during my travels.

I was honored with their stories—some of which had never been previously shared, even with the closest of friends. These connections have changed me personally and have given me the opportunity to see the world through the eyes of those I encountered. Through these conversations, my picture of success changed and I began to connect core themes to living an extraordinary life. It is through these experiences that I discovered eight secrets for Goal-Free Living.

Getting Started
in Goal-Free Living

Setting the Stage
for Goal-Free Living

I dread success. To have succeeded is to have finished one's business on earth, like the male spider, who is killed by the female the moment he has succeeded in courtship. I like a state of continual becoming, with a goal in front and not behind.

—*George Bernard Shaw*

$\mathcal{E}$arl Nightingale, chairman of Nightingale-Conant and personal development leader, once explained that there are two types of people: river people and goal people. Chuck Frey, founder of innovationstools.com, whom I met during my travels across the United States, provided this perspective on the differences between these types of people:

> Most of us are undoubtedly familiar with goal people. They are the individuals who write down their objectives and timetables for reaching them, and then focus on attaining them, one by one. By laying out a road map of future achievements in front of them, goal people give their creative minds a clear set of stimuli to work on. Their subconscious minds can then get to work incubating ideas and insights that will help them to reach their goals.
>
> River people, on the other hand, don't like to follow such a

structured route to success. They are called river people because they are happiest and most fulfilled when they are wading in a rich river of interest—a subject or profession about which they are very passionate. While they may not have a concrete plan with measurable goals, river people are often successful because they are so passionate about their area of interest. This, in turn, helps them to recognize breakthrough opportunities that may not even be visible on the mental radar screens of the more narrowly focused goal people. River people are explorers, continually seeking out learning opportunities and new experiences. For river people, joy comes from the journey, not from reaching the destination—exactly the opposite of goal people. From the standpoint of creativity, river people are more likely to benefit from serendipity, because they tend to be more open to new ideas, points of view, and insights than single-minded, focused goal people.

River people are individuals who live life out of experience rather than achievement. People driven by passion. These are the goal-free people. Goal-free people don't necessarily live a life free from all goals. They live free from the stranglehold of goals that grips so many people. They live experientially in each moment. A life of *their* design rather than that which society tells them to live. They have a deep appreciation for where they are today; they avoid worrying about the future.

Goal-Free Living is just that—living for the moment rather than achieving some future goal. It's about enjoying where you are now and having the life you want. Now. One of the people I met on my trip shared something that was counterintuitive to my earlier beliefs about goals. Dr. Doug Gardner, a former sports psychology consultant to the Boston Red Sox, said to me, "Goals can actually demotivate players in sports. When your focus is on hitting specific performance targets such as a batting average, you often underperform. This is especially true when you fail to hit your targets, even if your lack of success was due to factors outside of your control. The stress of having to perform creates a vicious cycle. The best players are less focused on numbers and are able to take one swing at a time. They are in the moment." Not something you typically would hear about sports, right? That's what I thought at first but it makes sense. When you focus on the moment, all the other noise goes away and you're able to really be with that experience. This is Goal-Free Living.

The Future as Context

Living goal-free requires a powerful context. Context is not a place to get to; it is something that changes your attitude and perception today. It is a mindset. To experience the power of context, imagine that as you read this, your phone rings. You answer the phone and the person on the other end notifies you that you won the raffle you entered last month. You and your family are going on an all-expenses-paid trip to Hawaii sometime next year. You jump for joy and become energized—now. Although this vacation is many months in the future, it changes your attitude today. This vacation hasn't happened. It isn't even real yet. However, thinking about and planning your vacation gives you pleasure long before the actual travel date. Often, the days just prior to your vacation are so exciting that you can hardly contain yourself. Imagine your last day at work before taking a two-week trip to a tropical island. Life looks completely different. All of your worries are gone. You may even be singing and dancing in the office. The thought of this exciting future makes today exciting.

Unfortunately for many people, the anticipation leading up to the vacation is more fun than the time away. Often the vacation itself rarely lives up to your expectations. Your excitement has you build up the perfect trip in your mind, one that could never exist. Even worse, when your vacation is over, you return to your normal life at work. You may feel worse than you did before you left because you have seen the light and long for those happy vacation times once again.

Now, imagine your future as a big and bold vacation. A vacation that is so exciting that you can hardly contain yourself now. A vacation that has you in action and playing hard every day. This is a vacation that you will never take. This is a vacation whose day will never come. Its sole purpose is to generate passion in your life today. A context. Something that calls you forward without defining a specific destination.

This context goes by many names. Purpose. Intention. Dream. Your calling. I use the word aspiration. With an aspiration, your actions and beliefs are no longer driven by societal norms, a desire for money or status, or arbitrary goals. Rather they are based on meaning found deep within your soul. This makes your existence more intense and alive with purpose. Goal-Free Living is about listening to your gut, trusting that you are moving in the right direction, a direction that has meaning for you. You take risks and try new things. You play full out. Everything you do fits with your purpose.

As Albert Einstein once said to describe his theory of relativity, "When you sit with a nice girl for two hours, it seems like two minutes. When you sit on a hot stove for two minutes, it seems like two hours." The challenges we face in life are relative. When you follow your aspiration, everything feels easy as it is in line with who you really are. This makes life more enriching.

Aspirations and Goals

There is much truth in the expression, "It's the journey, not the destination." Goals represent only the destination; somewhere to get to. That destination, in the goal-setting world, is often defined by the acronym SMART—Specific, Measurable, Achievable, Results-Oriented, and Time-Based. Goals represent a clearly defined end point, not the adventure in getting there. As Alan Watts, a great philosopher, once said, "Increasingly, our world consists of destinations and goals, with the times and spaces in between them eliminated by jet propulsion. Consequently, there is little satisfaction in reaching the goal, since a life full of end points is like trying to abate one's hunger by eating merely the precise ends of a banana" (*Nature, Man and Woman*, Vintage Books). Goals are not about satisfaction. In fact, the origin of the word "goal" comes from the Old English word *gol*, which means obstacle or boundary and is related to the word *gælan*, which means "to hinder." In order to achieve a goal, you must overcome barriers and roadblocks.

Conversely, look up "aspiration" and you will find that its origins are similar to those of the words "spirit" and "inspire." They are all derived at some level from the Latin word *aspirare*, which means "to breathe upon." Probably the connotation is "to breathe life into" or "panting with desire." Quite simply put, goals are logical, planned, and left-brain oriented. Aspirations, on

8

the other hand, are emotional, intuitive, experiential, and right-brain oriented.

We need both. Goals without aspirations often lead to despair. There is potential success, but a lack of passion. One person I met said, "I wrote down 20 goals a number of years back and have achieved them all. Now I feel worse than before." Achieving your goals does not mean you will achieve happiness. Equally, aspirations without any goals may lead to aimlessness. The key is to have the right balance of goals and aspirations, and to have the right relationship to your goals.

The Power of Goals and Aspirations

We often use the word goal synonymously with aspirations, purpose, and dreams. However, the difference between them can be the difference between life and death. Aspirations help us to find meaning through a sense of purpose. Something larger than ourselves.

During my travels I met Alepho Deng, someone whose personal story is a touching and powerful example of goals and aspirations—and of why both are needed. Alepho lives in an impoverished area of Southern California that seems light-years away from the ocean and wealth of San Diego only a few miles distant. I met with him at the small apartment he shared with a few other young men. Standing six feet tall, Alepho's physique gave the appearance of strength and confidence. From his self-assured exterior, I would never have imagined the heart-wrenching experiences he had lived through.

Alepho came to the United States only a few years ago.

9

What he had endured before arriving in the states was incredible. He recalled the situation of his childhood. In 1982 a civil war broke out in his home country, Sudan, in Africa. There was an attempt to overthrow the government, and a massive genocide ensued. Alepho was from the Dinka tribe. His tribe did not have any guns—they only had spears for hunting. The rebels attempting to overthrow the Sudanese government eventually made it to his village, where they burned everything and took the cattle and goats. The next day they returned to kill the tribesmen. (To date, over two million lives have been claimed by this conflict.) Alepho continued his story, "The attack was so brutal that we couldn't stay. So we left the village in search of a safer place to live. We eventually joined 17,000 other boys, some as young as five years old, who became known as The Lost Boys. We wandered the desert for three months non-stop. We lived off the land. It was cold in the middle of the night. The wild animals—lions, hyenas, and snakes—killed many of the boys. We weren't walking anywhere in particular. We just wanted to find somewhere safe to live. We wandered over a thousand miles to Ethiopia before being driven back toward Sudan. We shuffled around to stay alive. But everywhere we went was not safe. Boys were getting killed. So we moved on. Eventually we ended up in a UN-supported refugee camp in Kenya for eight years. There, we survived on one meal a day. It was horrible, but I knew that I could survive this since I survived Sudan." Fortunately, in 2001 with the help of the United States government and a number of charitable organizations, Alepho and 3,600 other Lost Boys were airlifted and resettled in various cites around the United States.

All of the Lost Boys had a goal. Survival. For many, this was the only conceivable goal. But as a goal, it was insufficient. I asked Alepho why so many others died, yet he survived. He responded, "I survived because I had a sense of purpose. I didn't want to live for the sake of living. I wanted to live so that I could make a difference in the world. I felt that if I could survive, I could use this experience—a learning experience—to make an impact in the lives of others. This sense of purpose kept me alive. Those who did not have this, perished." Today Alepho is living that aspiration and inspiring others by speaking at civic events, writing books, and helping others who are in need.

Goal-Free versus Goal-Focused

Aspirations breathe life into what we do. They are not somewhere to get to. Rather they are the context for creating a powerful existence today. It is fine to support your aspirations with small doses of goals. Sometimes you need to oscillate in and out of goal-free and goal-focused modes of operation. The key is, when you are in goal mode, be sure to relate to your goals in a healthy manner.

YOUR OWN GOALS, NOT THOSE OF SOCIETY

Goals are often not our own. According to my Goalaholic survey, over 50 percent of the population believes that they are living their lives in a way that satisfies others (friends, family, coworkers) more than it satisfies them. Many more are blind to this situation. We subconsciously absorb stimuli from the media, friends, and family, and unwittingly tailor our lives to conform to their norms. Goals should represent *your* values and *your* dreams rather than someone else's vision for your future. How does a goal make you feel? Do you get a rush of excitement? Does it make you want to wake up early in the morning to get started? If so, that's great. Some mild anxiety is normal, but if your stomach is churning and this goal seems like more work than it is worth, reconsider it. Choose goals that support your life values and aspirations.

HAPPINESS TODAY, NOT WAITING FOR THE FUTURE

According to my Goalaholics survey, 61 percent of the population find themselves saying that *they will be happy when . . . (fill in the blank).* They are willing to sacrifice today for the future. The key thing about Goal-Free Living is that it is about being in the moment and not about waiting for the future. A graduate school student who read my web site wrote me and said, "I was checking out the web site on your book and it inspired me. Last semester I found myself complaining about school a lot, even saying how I felt like I was sacrificing my present enjoyment of life for my future. But, what I realized was that I really did want to be in school and it is the right thing for me to be doing. Therefore I decided to adjust my attitude toward it, to take advantage of and enjoy the opportunities, learning, and growth it offers. And it's been going very well so far!" Sometimes you only need to change your attitude toward your goals to move them from goal-focused to goal-free.

PASSION, NOT HEDONISM

Goals driven by passion are not the same as goals driven by self-indulgence. Hedonistic tendencies, such as excessive partying, drugs, or materialism, are superficial and result only in fleeting moments of happiness. These behaviors and superficial wants do not tap into something deep within your soul. Goal-Free Living brings the focus onto your passions. Your purpose. It is about finding something with real meaning in your life, playing hard, having fun, being responsible, and being in action.

PLANNING, NOT PLANS

Goal-Free Living does require preparation and planning. As Igor Stravinsky, the Russian composer, noted, "Inspiration that falls on the unprepared and untrained mind is lost." You need to submit to the discipline of training and practice. Without it you cannot expect to benefit from inspiration. Although planning, preparation, and training sometimes involve goals, these can certainly be exciting present-time activities. They can be vigorous, imaginative, and creative. If planning itself is not exciting and invigorating, then it is probably a goal-focused activity. Conversely, playing with possibility too much can lead to stagnation. The key is to avoid becoming a planning addict where you never move out of the planning stages and into execution.

Use goals sparingly and have a healthy relationship to them. I prefer to think of these "healthy" goals as "paths," different roads on which we travel that move us forward with purpose. They help us make progress while keeping us free to enjoy the ride.

Is This Book a Goal?

Some people have asked me, "Isn't getting a book published a goal?" In the context of my aspiration, it is not. It is only one potential path supporting my aspiration. My interest lies in getting the word out about Goal-Free Living and to have fun in the process. If the book did not get published, there would be other paths: self-publishing, creating a magazine, a web site, or some new medium. Since its original conception this book has taken more than two years to complete. Had it been a goal, I might have forced it down a particular path to get it to press quickly. Instead I allowed it to mature and evolve, and to turn into something better. Something far beyond the original concept—a book on creativity (see the Setting Your Compass chapter for more details). People often confuse the means with the end. The book is a means, not the end. This book became a traditional goal for me only when I signed the contract with my publisher. Then they gave me deadlines and other requirements necessary for getting the book in stores on time. Even then, I still maintained a healthy relationship to the writing; I was enjoying the process.

Aspirations evolve and change over time. What you choose as your direction is not important, as long as it is something that gets you excited today. Remember, aspirations are inspirational. The path forward is an adventure. I have no plans and I have no idea how things will turn out. That is okay. Life will unfold naturally while taking this trip. I know I am never lost because I am living for the moment.

What Does Goal-Free Living Feel Like?

A life without absolutely any goals may not be desirable or even possible. But since goals often have such a hold on so many people, consider for a moment a life without goals. What would it look like for you? Go to the extreme. Think about it. Imagine the burden of struggling to achieve a future success being lifted from your shoulders. Imagine enjoying every moment of every day. What does it look like? How does it feel? Imagine your life just going with the flow. Imagine playing with possibility and making your dreams a reality. And now, after you've played with this for awhile, slowly start to add back in the goals—only the goals that truly empower you. Create a powerful aspiration so that these goals are fun and exciting. Don't plan the next step. Rather let it evolve and enjoy the process. Meander and weave through life.

Now you have a sense of Goal-Free Living. So lift the burden and enjoy life now. If (as Joseph Campbell used to say) "you follow your bliss," you'll have your bliss, regardless of the circumstances.

The Eight Secrets for Goal-Free Living

How do you make Goal-Free Living a reality in your life? During my travels around the world, I uncovered eight secrets that can help you create a goal-free life. Eight secrets that will help you live a more passionate and creative life today.

SECRET #1: USE A COMPASS, NOT A MAP

Through your experiences, your skills, and your values, find your passions. Use these as the compass for choosing a direction to take in life, without defining a specific destination. Avoid mapping out your life. Instead, allow it to take twists and turns and to evolve over time. Live in the moment while creating many paths of possibilities.

SECRET #2: TRUST THAT YOU ARE NEVER LOST

There are no right or wrong decisions in life. Just decisions. And there are no failures in life, only opportunities for growth. Taking a detour is not bad. Every seemingly wrong turn is a chance to learn and have new experiences.

SECRET #3: REMEMBER THAT OPPORTUNITY KNOCKS OFTEN, BUT SOMETIMES SOFTLY

Constantly watch for new opportunities that present themselves in unexpected ways. Keep your mind clear of clutter, expand your focus, and allow subtle messages to appear. Some of the best opportunities appear in unlikely places. On the road of life, be on the lookout for hidden signposts—as well as those that are right there in front of you.

SECRET #4: WANT WHAT YOU HAVE

Have a deep appreciation of where and who you are today. Rather than yearning for more out of your life, cherish the moment. Enjoy the view that life has given you, whether it's an ocean view or a parking lot view. When you measure your life by your own yard-stick, you realize what really matters to you.

SECRET #5: SEEK OUT ADVENTURE

People who live extraordinary lives tend to have a wide range of experiences. When possible they travel to new locations, rotate jobs (or positions), try new hobbies, and think like explorers. Diverse experiences can enrich your view of the world. Every day offers a chance to explore and discover. While you certainly don't need to travel the world, you can approach your life as an adventure. Every day.

SECRET #6: BECOME A PEOPLE MAGNET

Constantly attract, build, and nurture relationships with new people so that you have the support and camaraderie of others. Meet new people and take responsibility for the next steps after a connection is made. Creative ideas that are not implemented (and valued) are worthless.

SECRET #7: EMBRACE YOUR LIMITS

We are all human. As such we have a shadow side that we try to hide from the rest of the world. Rather than fighting, avoiding, or denying these limits, embrace them as a source of power. Realize that they are a part of you. Look at them as attributes rather than deficits. When you do, your inadequacies no longer control you; they connect you with the rest of us.

SECRET #8: REMAIN DETACHED

One characteristic that distinguishes a traditional goal from an aspiration or path is detachment. With a traditional goal you truly
desire a successful outcome. You are mentally and emotionally
involved with the result. With an aspiration you are committed to
the moment yet detached from the outcome. You do not worry
about whether or not your aspirations are even achievable. In fact
you know that the biggest and boldest aspirations may never become reality. And that's fine, because they provide a powerful
context that energizes you now.

These are the eight secrets that can help you live a goal-free
and passion-filled life. They are described in the following chap-
ters. They are, admittedly, quite simple and, in hindsight, somewhat obvious. Some are easy to implement now—seeking out
adventure doesn't require much effort; it just requires a bit of intention to make it happen. Others take practice—remaining detached is probably the most difficult to master because as human
beings we really want what we want. But with time and commitment, you can master these eight secrets in a way that will create a
powerful new mode of living.

How to Read This Book

At times, the concepts in this book may seem countercultural and
go against what you have been taught in the past. This may make it
hard for you to truly believe that what I am presenting here is desirable, let alone possible. Being skeptical is good. In fact, if you

agree with everything you read, you are either already living goal-free or you aren't thinking critically enough about the concepts. While reading this, in the back of your mind you should be thinking *"yes, but"* quite frequently. *"Yes,* the concept is appealing, *but* how can I live this way when I have responsibilities to a spouse and children?" *"Yes,* this may work for someone with money, *but* I am living hand to mouth and can't afford to change my job." *"Yes,* this may work for free-spirited individuals, *but* I need structure and predictability in my life." *"Yes,* this is interesting, *but* isn't it really just a matter of semantics?" As you read the book, list out your *"yes, buts."* They are useful as they help identify limitations you subconsciously place on your life. These limiting beliefs, which incidentally are not real, are what will stop you from living a goal-free and passion-filled life. So be critical, but stay open to new viewpoints.

Just as there is no right or wrong way to live your life, there is no right or wrong way to read this book. Feel free to read the secrets in order or skip around. Skim some sections, delve deeply into others. The secrets are not linear or mutually exclusive. In any case, don't just read this book. Make a commitment to digesting it, questioning it, and applying it. Small changes today in your life can have a huge impact in the future. And they will almost certainly have a huge impact on your attitude today. At the end of each secret is a section on "making it happen." This summarizes the secret and provides specific actions and questions to help you move forward.

After the eight secrets, there is a chapter, Setting Your Compass, which tells the real story behind my cross-country trip and provides a useful metaphor for Goal-Free Living. Next, the epilogue, is one individual's account of her transformation from goalaholism to being goal-free. This powerful story clearly illustrates how goals can be detrimental to relationships, health, and success.

Appendix A contains the answers to some frequently asked questions. Some people may want to start reading the book there. In Appendix B, our "Are You a Goalaholic?" quiz appears. In addition to scoring your quiz in Appendix C, you can compare your answers to those of more than 1,000 respondents (Appendix D).

If people are to have one goal, it should be to live a passionate and fulfilling life. But treating that as a goal—as with any goal—would destroy the joy of the journey. Instead let life unfold. When you free yourself from the burden that goals can create, you will find yourself in an unpredictable world filled with possibility and excitement. A world where creativity flows naturally, new opportunities appear around every corner, and success finds you—effortlessly. Living goal-free will lead to the creation of a new, unrecognizable, and more powerful you.

The Eight Secrets of Goal-Free Living

Use a Compass, Not a Map

If the world were merely seductive, that would be easy. If it were merely challenging, that would be no problem. But I arise in the morning torn between a desire to improve (or save) the world and a desire to enjoy (or savor) the world. This makes it hard to plan the day.

—*E. B. White*

Sometimes maps can be useful. They help us get from point A to point B as directly and as efficiently as possible. But life is not about efficiency. It is about exuberance. You can't map out passion. Maps become restrictive when we rely on them too heavily to guide our every move. Using a map is fine. But just because you possess one does not mean you need to detail every mile of your journey.

This secret is about finding a direction in life that feels right, something big and bold that calls you forward into action. This means finding something that inspires you. Rather than mapping out your travels in detail, you explore, meander, and weave. You try new things, set your themes, and venture into an unknown, uncharted, and unplanned future. You must have the courage to be willing to change directions often, finding new paths along the way. Just as with my trip across the United States, sometimes the best discoveries are made when you have a sense of purpose but no plans. So instead of a map, I suggest you use a compass. Have a sense of direction in life, and then move forward experientially.

Find Your Compass Setting

To ditch the map and follow your compass, you need to determine what your particular setting should be. So how do you find your aspiration, your own sense of purpose? How do you know if the direction you are going is the right one for you? Finding your compass setting is about balancing passion, skills, and value. Here is a simple litmus test you can use to determine if you have all of these necessary elements to find your compass setting and follow it.

- *Passion:* Do you choose paths that are based on your dreams, hopes, and aspirations? These comprise your compass. What did you enjoy doing as a child? What have you often thought about doing but have said, "I don't have enough time or money?" What have you believed in your heart was your passion, but others told you was a crazy idea? What is a hobby or interest you have that could be transformed into a career? What would you do if money were not an issue? Look deep inside yourself. Go beyond what you think you *should* be doing as a responsible adult, and find what you really *want* to do with your life.
- *Skills:* You need to have or acquire the necessary skills to make things happen. What are you good at? What are you willing to learn? Who else could you involve to complement your skills?

- *Value:* You need to offer something that the world needs and values. Value works two ways. One is the value you receive, whether it be monetary compensation, or personal satisfaction. You need to be able to live, so making money is important. It doesn't need to be a great deal, but it needs to be enough to support your lifestyle. Are you willing to change your lifestyle to have a life you love? How can you make money at your chosen endeavor? The other value is the value you give, the contribution you make to others. Most people have been conditioned to check for what's in it for them in any situation. The key is to remember that once you focus on becoming something, receiving happens automatically. If you want to receive a higher compensation, you have to become a person delivering higher value.

The ideal life is one where you have all three: passion, skills, and value. Think about your life. Look at your chosen profession. Are you doing something that addresses all three dimensions? If so, congratulations. Keep experiencing, evolving, and adapting. Or maybe you don't know the answer to these questions. That's okay. Either way there are things you can do to set, test, and improve your compass.

Try New Things

Many people try to intellectualize what they want to do with their lives. They create spreadsheets with lists of pros and cons, likes and dislikes. They take classes and workshops where they sit and think about their life. But sometimes it is difficult to intellectual-ize passion. Passion is something you have to experience. Many people I meet say, "I would change careers if only I knew what to do." Without this sense of direction they are stuck. How do you get unstuck? Get out and explore, try new things, meet new peo-ple—live your life through each experience. When you do this, you will discover (and experience) activities that you like and ones that you do not like. Then use your passion as a barometer to help determine which direction to turn. Do more of the things that you like and less of the things that you don't.

Through experiential living, you will encounter in real time, the course you should take, just as Mark Grossman has done throughout his life. As a 13-year-old boy, Mark watched a PBS special on how kids his age were making cartoons with 8-mm film. He was inspired. He ran to his father and said, "Daddy, this looks interesting. Can I do it?" Being supportive, his father pulled an old 8-mm camera off the top shelf of the closet. He dusted it off and handed it to Mark. "Here, son, have fun." Mark held the camera in his hands, knowing that he was going to be a great film-maker some day. Knowing that, he went on to fulfill his dreams.

Thirty-five years later, this young boy is a husband, a father—and is selling giant menorahs as lawn ornaments. How did this as-piring filmmaker stray so far from his childhood dream? Actually, he didn't. He followed his dream—to be who he really is and to do what he loves to do, regardless of the direction it takes him.

Mark Grossman thought he wanted to be a filmmaker. He earned a Bachelor of Fine Arts in Film Making from the School of Visual Arts in New York and a Masters degree in Communica-tion Arts from the New York Institute of Technology (NYIT). His career progressed through his early twenties but he soon realized that if he wanted to continue he would have to relocate to the West Coast, a move he did not want to make. Instead, he taught at NYIT for a few years until he had his fill of academia.

Next he accepted a position in advertising and marketing at Norelco, while at the same time selling himself to the manager of a new local cable television station as the right guy to start up their community programming studio. He got the job a year later and won awards for his work. Always wanting to try new things, he simultaneously pursued an interest in politics. "I always seem to have many balls in the air," he notes.

The political vocation took shape when a number of Democrats won key positions on Long Island and new opportunities opened up for him. He was offered the regional representative position for New York Governor Mario Cuomo. "I wasn't sure I had the right skills," he says, "but I always joked that politics and show business are one and the same." His training in filmmaking proved perfect for government because his role with the governor was largely about communications. He served six years, until Cuomo lost re-election in 1994. That marked the end of his life in government.

After feeling sorry for himself—for one day—Grossman started his own public relations business, focusing on the government sector. After two months he had enough commitments from clients to equal his former income. In 10 years the business grew to seven employees.

Now he is ready to move on again. His next venture? Most likely it will be selling giant menorahs for display on people's lawns—much like Christmas trees. He explains the latest twist in his colorful career: "My wife is Catholic and I am Jewish. We have a 60-foot blue spruce that we would light up every year in conjunction with our local civic association. The tree is the centerpiece of the community during the holidays each year. But I felt I needed some equal time, so about five years ago I built an 8-foot-wide, 6-foot-tall menorah so it could stand prominently next to the tree. I made it out of PVC pipes, electric wires, and flicker-flame bulbs."

The menorah was featured in local newspapers, and individuals expressed an interest in buying one. He now owns the domain name Giantmenorah.com, and has found a distributor. "Ten years is the longest I have done anything," he says with pride. "In some respects this menorah project is a logical extension of what I have done in the past. It will take advantage of my PR background. I will be the marketer, not the manufacturer. Will it be successful? Who knows? But I am having fun moving forward with the idea."

What is Mark Grossman getting out of his unpredictable life? "Simple," he says. "I want to be as healthy as I can be. I want my kids to be smart and healthy. I want a good relationship with my wife. I want to continue to make a decent living. Are these goals? I don't think so. They are not detailed. I don't have any predefined notion of what the future looks like."

One of his criteria has been to choose endeavors that give him great personal satisfaction. "My best moments have been when I felt part of something bigger than myself," he says. "Regardless of what I have done, my freedom has always taken me to places I enjoyed, at least for the time that I was there. I want my kids to have that same opportunity to try and experience many things."

Throughout the years, a common thread in Mark's life has been his love of PR and the visual arts. This has served him well. What is your aspiration? Ask yourself what is something you could try right now that might be in the context of your aspiration—and even if it isn't, try something new anyway. If you've never really cooked before, make a meal. Take a walk outside, change your surroundings. Maybe there's a new project at work coming up; volunteer to be on the team. What is something you've always wanted to do but have never tried? Try it today.

Set Themes, Not Resolutions

One way of living more experientially is to avoid making "resolutions." You know, the thing we all do on New Year's Eve. Think about it. What have been your resolutions in the past? Lose 15 pounds? Quit smoking? Run a marathon? Save more money? Get a new job?

Most resolutions have specific, measurable results to achieve. They are also time-based; you have only until the end of the year to achieve your objectives. New Year's resolutions are often nothing more than SMART goals. And we know how successful most people are in sticking to their resolutions. In fact, according to my survey, only 8 percent of Americans say they successfully achieve their resolutions.

Rather than resolutions, choose one word to describe the next year. It serves as a theme for the year rather than a specific goal. For a colleague of mine, this year is about "service," serving others in whatever way she can to make a contribution. For another person, this year is about "flow," making the year effortless. For a friend who is going through a divorce and change of career, his theme is "new beginnings."

C. Leslie Charles, a fellow professional speaker, and Rob, her partner of 30 years, have had an annual ritual since 1995 around setting their theme. She says, "My book, *Why Is Everyone So*

Cranky? may not have happened without our practice of annual themes. It was during our Year of Exploration that I decided to 'explore my potential as a writer' and embark on this daunting project. In the following year, our Year of Adventure, the book was published. The Year of Lightness that followed helped me maintain my perspective in the heat of an extended media blitz."

Their ritual starts on the winter solstice of each year (December 21), when Leslie and Rob reflect on the previous year. They look at what they accomplished; the ups and the downs. It is a chance to appreciate the past and each other. They begin discussing the next year, formulating some general thoughts on potential themes. Then on New Year's Eve they jointly choose their word for the next year. For them it is an integrating experience since they will have a shared theme. They choose words that motivate and empower them. And this has created surprising results. Things they could not have imagined via traditional goal-setting. Leslie has written books, launched a book editing business, and created an inspirational jewelry business. All were unpredictable, unplanned, and spectacularly successful.

My overarching aspiration at the moment is to "make a massive and visible impact in the world." To support this, my theme last year was "flexibility," creating a life style that allowed me to take many different paths. This year is about "platform" (defined as "a place, means, or opportunity for public expression of opinion"). It is about creating a foundation that enables me to make an impact with as many people as possible and creates a reputation that enables greater growth in the future. So when I am presented with several options, I think about my theme and choose the one that leads me in that direction. No planning required, and certainly no specificity in its design.

What is the one word you want to use to describe your next year? A good place to start is with your traditional resolutions. Then ask yourself why. Want to lose weight? Look at the reasons why. Do you want to be healthier? Do you want to have more confidence? If so, instead of dieting, "health" or "confidence" may be good themes. Choose a theme that is expansive, gets your juices flowing, has you excited, and moves you into action.

Still can't think of a theme? Refer back to your aspiration. What theme would support it? Passion, peace, love, friendship, travel, or self-expression? Or maybe new horizons, adventure, or mind expansion might be a good start. Don't worry if you haven't named your aspiration yet—it may come out of your theme. Rather than sitting around trying to figure out your passion, choose a direction that will enable you to experience it. If all else fails and you still can't figure out what your passion is, then make "finding your passion" your theme.

This is a simple compass setting. It does not dictate a specific outcome and does not imply a particular path or plan. Write your theme on a Post-It note and stick it on your computer screen. Write it on your bathroom mirror. Put it anywhere as a quick reminder of what you are about at this moment in time. Resolutions are things to do. Themes are a way to be.

Create Many Paths

Another way of living more experientially is to create many paths. Just like a tree that scatters many seeds not knowing or caring which ones will grow, we want to scatter many seeds of possibility without worrying about which ones will germinate and flourish.

We just know that some will. "Could do" lists are this chance to create possibility and find new paths.

One person I met during my travels uses this approach to living his own life. He does not try to plan and predict everything. He doesn't use to-do lists the way most people think of to-do lists. Rather, he puts everything that seems to matter into a "could do" list. Anything that gets him excited is put on this list. If he thinks it is something he might be interested in doing some time in the future, it goes on the list. If a concept fails to continue to inspire him, he crosses it off his list, even if he never achieves it. By playing with possibility, he gets himself excited today without concern for which seeds will sprout. He keeps the juiciest concepts right in front of him.

He is always recopying and rearranging his list. He says, "When I get tired, my core practice is to write out the list. This helps me from a coherence standpoint, giving me the ability to get in touch with what matters. If I get stuck and can't make progress, I will wait and rewrite the list another time. It is like playing solitaire. Throughout the game, you are constantly moving cards around. Then at some point, after going through the deck, you may not see any more moves. But you still go through each pile one last time just to see if there is a move that has eluded you. If there are no moves, it is time to shuffle the cards and play again. Sometimes, I put things on the list. Other times I let them fall off. I try and find connections between different items on the list, combining them into one item. Through this process I create many paths of possibility." The most important aspect of this process is that the list is called a "could do" list. Not a "to do," "must do," "should do," or "will do" list. It's not the number of things that we *could do* that creates stress in our lives. The source of stress is the things that we say we *will do* or feel we *should do*—and these are the things on most people's "to do" lists.

Think about possibility. Keep what matters right in front of you. Keep your "could do" list large and your "to do" list small. Then take action on the ideas that inspire you now and move them to your "to do" list. Your "could do" list is an expression and acknowledgement of your power. Your "to do" list is the willingness and commitment to use that power.

Sense Your Direction and Believe in It

To live experientially requires patience and courage. It also takes a strong belief that things will work out and a belief in yourself, regardless of the adversities and doubts you may encounter. Take the case of Preethi Nair, who came to England from India as a small child. Now in her 30s, she is a successful author and a laureate of the Asian Woman of Achievement Award in Britain. She has achieved this without any real plan. All she had was her aspiration—"a strong desire to be a writer." Her path toward success was certainly not linear. And it certainly wasn't easy as she stumbled along the way.

Preethi comes from a traditional Indian family that believes in success through good academic training, a professional qualification, and a big salary. So she started by earning two degrees and becoming a management consultant. She was miserable.

Her aspiration drove her to start writing her first book, working in the evenings and on weekends. Three years later the manuscript was finished and she sent copies to the major publishing houses.

Full of confidence, she walked into her boss's office and handed in her resignation.

As fate would have it, soon after her resignation the rejection slips from publishers flooded in. It seemed as though her dream would end quickly. Then she heard about self-publishing. Instead of getting royalties and advances for a book, the writer pays someone to print and publish it. "I took my life savings—£12,000 pounds ($20,000)—and put the whole amount down into self-publishing," she says. With the printer's help, her first novel, *Gypsy Masala*, was designed and produced.

She had 3,000 copies of her book printed and sent out 500 review copies to the press, leaving her with 2,500 copies. Not knowing what to do next, she wrangled a stall at the London Book Fair, one of the premier events for the book industry, and handed out hundreds more copies.

In the following weeks, reviews started to appear in the British media. Unfortunately none of her books were in shops. She had overlooked distribution. "I did not realize what it took to get a book into a bookstore," she says. So she personally went to more than 250 bookshops throughout London, dropping off books on consignment. Finally, one of the major book chains picked it up and made it their staff choice. In one shop alone it sold 3,000 copies. The chain wanted to stock the book in 40 of their branches, so Preethi ordered a second printing even though this meant going deeper into debt.

"Demand was soaring. Everything I was waiting for was handed to me at that moment. And then disaster. There was a major petrol [gasoline] crisis in England, where for four days all truckers were on strike. Nothing moved within the country. So when I was most heavily in demand, my books could not get delivered to the bookstores."

Her momentum hit a brick wall; opportunity had swiftly passed her by. Books were not selling and publishers were not calling. Exhausted, disheartened, jobless, and heavily in debt, she just wanted to give up. Instead she decided to give it one last try.

She called a woman she had met at the Book Fair, Lynda Logan (one of the original Calendar Girls) and explained the situation. Lynda agreed to give Preethi the use of her country house to write a second book, and said she would provide access to her literary agent. "I was so overwhelmed and inspired. I decided I would give it at least another six weeks. No matter what happened, I could at least say that I had done my very best." Preethi wrote her second book, *100 Shades of White*, in just four weeks. The agent loved it and took it to the publishers who had rejected her the first time around—and this time she was successful. HarperCollins gave her a three-book contract. Just a week after she signed with them, the BBC bought the rights to turn the new book into a 90-minute television adaptation.

"I could never, in hindsight, have planned any of this," Preethi recalls. "Bumbling in the dark may have been the only way I could have achieved the success I have. I am clear it was not a goal in the traditional sense. It was truly an intention. I only had a sense of direction and then operated from intuition and gut instinct rather than logic and plans."

Preethi is a perfect example of following her purpose, even in the face of uncertainty. Her strong belief in her aspiration is what allowed her to use creative thinking to move from opportunity to trauma to opportunity. With a clear sense of direction in mind, she moved forward without plans, without specific goals, and without an understanding of the process. And yet she was successful in achieving her dream.

Making It Happen

Maps are useful in trying to get to your destination as quickly and efficiently as possible. But life is not about efficiency. It is about exuberance. And you can't map out passion. Instead of relying on detailed maps, develop a sense of direction—a compass setting—and allow life to unfold naturally.

To help you apply the concepts of Use a Compass, Not a Map to your own life, take the time to review these practices and questions. Answer the questions for yourself. Revisit them from time to time. Use them to help you live experientially and avoid planning out a specific path. There are no right or wrong answers. Enjoy the journey. Have fun.

FIND YOUR COMPASS SETTING

Balance passion, skills and value.

- Discover your passion. Review the questions on pages 25–26. Then, look back on your life. What do you wish you would have done? If you could, what would you still like to do? If you could do one thing, what would that be? What dreams do you feel you have had to leave behind? What do you want to do before you die? What is something you would like to do that you don't think will ever happen? What are you interested in that never feels like work? What activities do you do where hours fly by yet it only feels like minutes? Make decisions based on your interests, not your checkbook or busy schedule.

- Get the skills. What are you known for being good at? How can you gain other necessary skills? What additional skills may be useful that are not traditionally considered? How can you differentiate yourself from others to help you stand out from the crowd? Who can you collaborate with to fill your skill gaps?

- Create value for yourself and others. How can you make a living at this? How can you help the world value your contribution? How can you creatively stay true to your passion while having the success you desire? How can you make a difference?

Once you choose the direction you will follow, check to see how you feel. Do you get a rush of excitement? Does it make you want to wake up early in the morning to get started? What does your gut tell you? Choose a direction where you feel part of something bigger than yourself.

TRY NEW THINGS

Avoid over-intellectualizing the direction in which you want to take your life; experience it. Go for it. Get out there and play. Tomorrow, try one new thing. Do things you have never done before, no matter how minor they are. Drive a different way to work. Try a new hobby. Read a different section of the newspaper. Then, do more of the things you like to do and less of the things that you don't. For more on "Trying New Things," see Secret #5, Seek Out Adventure.

SET THEMES, NOT RESOLUTIONS

Rather than set a resolution (i.e., a goal), choose one word to describe your next year. Choose something that is bold and broad. Ask yourself why you chose that theme. Is there any larger, more expansive theme you could choose? If you are stuck, try passion, peace, love, friendship, travel, or self-expression as a theme. Or, make "finding your passion" your theme for the year. Write your theme in a place where you will be constantly reminded. Remain open to new possibilities and to changes in direction at any point in the future

CREATE MANY PATHS

Rather than one path, create many paths on which to travel. Use "could do" lists rather than "to do" lists. Keep possibility in front of you. Keep your list of "could do" items large and your list of "to do" items small. Add and subtract from your "could do" list on a regular basis, based on what inspires you. I have my "could do" list on a flip chart in my living room. Put yours somewhere where you will view it often.

SENSE YOUR DIRECTION AND BELIEVE IN IT

Even if you are encountering obstacles, stick with your direction. You will hit roadblocks. Rather than get discouraged, learn from these experiences. Problem solving can be an invigorating process. Be creative. There is more than one way to solve a challenge. Sometimes "bumbling in the dark"—operating from intuition and gut instinct rather than logic and plans—is the best way to gain new experiences. And be sure to constantly reconnect with your passion along the way.

SECRET #2

Trust That You Are Never Lost

Sometimes on the way to your dream, you get lost and discover a better one.

> —*Jack Gallo (played by George Segal)*
> *on TV's* Just Shoot Me

I once gave a presentation on Goal-Free Living, and a woman in the audience asked a question: "I work in a cubicle in a well-known technology firm and I am unhappy. How do I know if it is me or if it is my job? Do I need to change myself or change my job?" I asked others in the audience for their answer to that question. Most people gave answers that hedged their bet. "Stay at your job while exploring other options," or "If you are really miserable, find another job quickly and quit this job," or the most creative, "Quit your job now. How could you work another day for the evil empire?"

My answer is very simple: *It doesn't really matter.* With the right mindset, you are never lost. If you believe that the path you are on is the right one, then it is. Quitting your job doesn't change things. You can change jobs all you like, but it won't matter if you don't have the right attitude. Conversely you can change your attitude and find new opportunities where you are today, without changing jobs.

Ignoring this secret led to my divorce. From the beginning, I was never really "in" my marriage to Beth Anne. I was too busy chasing my career goals to focus on the relationship. The relationship languished, and the two of us suffered. I could have chosen to commit to my marriage and make it work. Equally, I could have chosen to end it early on when it was clear it wasn't working. Either decision would have moved us forward somehow. Unfortunately, however, I did neither. The marriage dragged on for five years until Beth Anne ultimately made the decision for both of us.

Quite often in life we avoid issues that make us uncomfortable or afraid, and decide *not* to decide. Indecision is a no man's land with no direction and no progress. By consistently and confidently committing to a decision at the crossroads, you are never lost, because you will always have the power to change direction.

Avoid Decision Avoidance

Most people avoid making decisions in their lives. Should I change my job? Am I dating the right person, or should we break up? Should I buy a new house? Where should I go on vacation? What should I do with my life? These all seem like pretty big decisions. And for most people they are.

We think "Oh, it's so hard to make these big decisions," when what's really hard is the indecision. In life there are no right or wrong decisions. There are only decisions. When we come to a fork in the road, we tend to overanalyze it. We might say, "I have an opportunity to create this new business venture *but . . ."* So we end up staying on the same path. Or we may choose a particular path, but then rethink our decision. Remember the story of Sodom and Gomorrah? Those who left the city prior to its destruction were advised not to look back; if they did, they would turn into a pillar of salt.

There is a tendency to look back and think about having made the wrong decisions. Yet we all make the right decision given the information we have at the time, and whatever the outcome, that is the right decision. We can never know where the alternative decision would have taken us or how badly *that* route might have turned out. We need to stop looking back at our decisions and questioning whether we made the right move. Look forward and make your new path work for you. Now. Not forever, but in this moment. You can always move to a different path when so inspired. Movement in any direction is better than stagnation and indecision. As Yogi Berra once reportedly said, "When you come to a fork in the road, take it."

One of the reasons we worry so much and wonder whether we are on the right track is that we often see decisions as long term, semi-permanent decisions. If you are driving your car and you get onto a highway where there are no exits for 300 miles, you had better be certain that you are on the right road. Making the right decision is critical when you don't have any alternative paths on which to travel. Goals, as most people relate to them, are like hopping onto a road five-years-long with no exits. One road, no options, and lots of traffic. And since you typically choose a road with many potholes, the driving is hard work.

But what if you were on a beautiful winding country road where there are exits every mile, frequent intersections, and a rotary from time to time? What if you had many paths on which to travel, and from which to choose? Then making the right decision becomes less stressful, because you could always change direction. If you drove down a road like this, you would only have to plan to the next fork in the road. And if getting to your destination quickly is not important, then the good news is that you can never get lost. If this is how you treat your life, you will be more likely to enjoy the ride. Every detour is a new experience.

Commit to Your Happiness

One woman I know works for a major multinational company. She had been considering leaving for quite some time to pursue her passion for yoga and create wellness centers around the country, but she was worried about whether or not it was the right decision. Should she stay at work while pursuing her dream? Or should she quit? Maybe she should just wait for the right time to leave, when she had saved more money or had found a place for her wellness center. And then someone suggested that she create a wellness center at her company, creating it as an annex for employees. Her first reaction was that this would never work. She had, in her mind, already rejected that as a possibility. But then she decided to look into it, and in a conversation with an executive of her company she found that there might be interest in making this happen. She also discovered that in most large corporations there was a growing demand for these services. Instantly her enthusiasm for her wellness center, and for her company, soared. With her decision to take a first step (and not the first one she envisioned), she is now excited about staying in her job *and* creating a chain of company-based wellness centers. She has created an altogether different business strategy by changing her attitude toward work and by making a decision. Trusting that every move is the right move, either path—staying in her corporate job or leaving to start her wellness centers—works if she has the right mindset and takes action.

Remember that no matter what path you are on, you are on the right path. If you are enjoying it and playing it full out, then it's the right thing to do.

The Safe Way Is the Unsafe Way

There's an important distinction to make about this secret. Even though whatever path you're on is the right path, that doesn't necessarily mean you should stay on the path you are on. Goal-Free Living is not a reason to stay in an unsatisfying job, it's not about abdication, and it's not an excuse for not being successful. The key difference is your belief. If you believe you're on the right path, then you're going the right way. You can never get lost on the way to your aspiration, because your aspiration is not somewhere to get to. It is a compelling context for the way you live your life today. You can get lost if you are a goalaholic.

Living goal-free can feel risky. Not knowing what the future might hold can be uncomfortable. Giving up your safety net may seem unwise. We are brought up to want that safety net. We've been taught that having a "real" job no matter how unhappy we are at it, for example, is the safe thing to do—it's the way to live your life—when in fact that whole process stops you from living the life you want. When we have a safety net, it actually makes us play small.

What we often think is safe is not. A woman I know told me the story of her father and his safety net. Her father was an intelligent, well-educated, and hard-working man. He had worked for almost 20 years in the research department of a steel manufacturing company. He made good money and consistently moved his way up in his department, eventually becoming the manager of research. While the steel industry took hits over the years, his job seemed secure. Layoffs only happened in the steel mills, not in upper management. He liked the stability of his job but not his actual job. What he really wanted to do was teach and consult. After about 18 years at the steel company, he thought about starting his own consulting firm but he didn't want to lose his safety net. He did some consulting on the side while working his full-time job but he didn't really take his consulting business as far as it could go. Two years later, the steel company made major cuts in staff. He, along with most of the research department, was let go. So what he thought was safe, wasn't. Ironically—or maybe not— without his safety net, his consulting business began to soar.

As one person I interviewed said, "I find that having a safety net is so disempowering. That is what is scary. But it is so well disguised as the sensible and responsible thing to do that we just get sucked into following it. We worry too much about making the wrong decision. So we never make positive change in our lives." Fear of failure or making the wrong decision prevents action. Without action there is no progress. Ironically, many times we fear losing something that we don't even have. The safe way is really the unsafe way.

What You Focus On Expands

A key lesson to remember is, "What you focus on expands." If you focus on the possibility of making a wrong choice, you will find evidence to support a decision that may not feel like the right one. If you focus on the positive things in your life, and trust that you are on the right path, your brain will find evidence to support that belief. In the movie *The Santa Clause*, Tim Allen plays divorced toy maker Scott, whose son, Charlie, is spending Christmas Eve with him. During the night, Charlie hears a noise on his roof. He wakes up his father, who takes a look. He sees Santa Claus himself on the roof, although he doesn't recognize him. Scott calls for him and Santa trips and, sadly, dies. Scott puts on Santa's red suit, and the next thing he knows he has turned into Santa himself, putting on weight, growing a big gray beard, and visiting the North Pole. While at the North Pole he encounters a small female elf who shows him around. The new Santa is amazed. He looks down at the elf and says, "I see it, but I don't believe it." The diminutive elf looks up at him and explains that that is the problem with adults. They wait until they see something before they believe it. Children, on the other hand, live magical lives because they believe things, and therefore they see them. The same is true in our everyday lives. If we believe we have taken the right path, we will begin to see the opportunities and the reasons why it was the right decision. Believing is seeing. And this can be applied to even the most mundane decisions we make.

Once I attended a weekend-long workshop on how to design experiential workshops. This class was taught at a yoga and spiritual center, which made me a bit nervous since I have never done yoga, don't meditate, and do not generally subscribe to "new age" practices. Upon arrival, I found that many of the people were dressed in Bohemian type garb, hardly the business casual attire I had grown accustomed to. The rooms had the feel of a glorified college dormitory. I quickly learned that all meals were vegetarian, there was no talking during breakfast, and there would be a dance in the afternoon where everyone hops around to the beat of African drums. What did I get myself into? Had I made a bad decision by signing up for this course?

When I went to my class the first evening we did some unusual things—at least for me—such as dancing, chanting, and meditating. As the instructor put it, these were "experiences." That they were. However, I struggled to see how these "experiences" had anything to do with designing a workshop. The next morning it was more of the same. I found myself becoming more frustrated and stressed. I reached the point where I debated leaving the class. Why waste my time on something that was not helping me design experiential workshops? That was the reason I was there. That's when it dawned on me. I was treating the workshop like a goal. I believed I was there for a specific reason and I had a preconceived notion of what the workshop should look like. Because of that I became myopically focused. As long as I was questioning whether I had made the right decision, I could not be present and learn whatever there was to learn.

I decided to give up the goal of "learning how to design experiential workshops." I accepted that I was on the right path at that moment. Rather than complain and be miserable, I instantly changed my focus to getting as much out of the weekend as possible. In the end it was a truly wonderful weekend. I enjoyed the class. I met incredible people, had amazing conversations, and learned many important things including (ironically) how to design experiential workshops. I learned in ways that were different than I had expected. This would not have happened if learning how to design workshops had remained a goal. Sometimes even the smallest goals can be detrimental to our happiness and success. It's a matter of believing that the path you are on is the right one. If you truly believe you are in the wrong place, either change your attitude and get the most out of the situation—or leave. Whether you stay or go, commit to your chosen path. Be sure to look around and learn a few things along the way.

Listen to a Silent Mind

How do you shift your focus? How can you trust that the path you are on is the right one for you? There is no easy answer, but there are ways to help you hear your inner voice, that part of your mind that knows the real you: your likes, dislikes, and passions. The word *Mushin* is used extensively in Japan. It means silent mind, empty mind. A mind that is void of thought patterns and mental chatter. The ability to listen to that inner voice is critical on the journey to self-awareness. It is said that Aristotle used to lie in bed with a ball in his hand so that when he fell asleep the ball would drop and bang a copper plate below. The noise would wake him up, keeping him in a state of mingled sleep and consciousness. This is when he generated his best ideas and insights.

One of the people I interviewed during my travels, Doug Stevenson from Chicago, Illinois, told me of a similar situation he once personally encountered. "One night in college I was agonizing over a paper I was writing about Norman Mailer and Truman Capote. I wanted to describe a new type of writing that was a hybrid of journalism and fiction. I struggled for hours, thinking it through, but could not put anything coherent or interesting on paper. Then I remember having this flash of insight at 3 A.M. I had been working on it for so long that my logical left brain went to sleep. That's when my creative right brain woke up—or at least it started to speak loud enough to be heard. My mind exploded and I wrote the perfect paragraph that summed up the entire paper. From there, the paper was born quickly and effortlessly. Once my rational self left the room, everything came together quickly."

To tap into this inner voice, there is a simple technique you can try. It does not require a therapist, a counselor, or a consultant. It requires only you and a tape recorder. Sit in a quiet, comfortable location, one where you can hear and listen to your innermost thoughts without distraction. Dim the lights. When you are relaxed, breathe deeply, turn on your tape recorder, and talk. Talk about the thoughts in your head. Talk about how you are feeling at that moment. Talk about the things that upset you, or the things that you enjoy doing. Talk about your hobbies, your friends, your passions. Keep talking, exploring as much territory as possible. Talk about things you would like to do. Things you have dreamed about. Things you wished you had done as a kid. Things about the world that frustrate you. Talk about anything. Don't filter what you say. Talk about taboo subjects like politics, religion, or sex. There are no right or wrong answers. There are no right or wrong topics. Just let it flow.

After you have talked as long as you can, rewind the tape and play it back. Listen to the entire tape. Listen to your words. More importantly, listen to your intonation, volume, and enthusiasm. In listening to yourself, you will discover the areas where you are most passionate. If you are excited you speak more quickly, maybe a bit louder, and certainly more energetically. You may find that you sound calm, slow, and relaxed when talking about other subjects. These may also be passions for you, areas of your life where you feel centered. As you are listening, jot down the things you said that you think best represent the areas of your life where you are most passionate. In some cases, a source of passion may be stirred by anger or frustration.

Some people may find that this exercise is easier to do with a friend. It can be done over the phone or in person. Your friend can ask you questions, facilitating the conversation, or he can just listen. Sometimes just having another person there who is actively listening, but not speaking, can help your thoughts flow. (You may also want to return the favor, doing the same for him.) Through this process, you can become clearer about where your interests lie. This will give you confidence in choosing a path and knowing that you are on the right path wherever you are.

All Paths Are Equal, but Some Paths Are More Equal Than Others

In the novel *Animal Farm*, George Orwell wrote, "All animals are equal, but some animals are more equal than others." Orwell's grim perspective notwithstanding, his point is quite true. The Goal-Free Living (and more optimistic) version of this concept is "All paths are equal, but some paths are more equal than others." Many of us often find ourselves on paths that bring us success in certain areas of our life. But this success may keep us from recognizing opportunities in other important areas. Always be open to the possibility of an even *more right* path. Remember that when something doesn't seem right, it probably isn't. Learn to ask yourself forward-thinking questions and trust your inner voice, because it never lies.

For one person, listening to this inner voice was the source of his future success. During my consulting years I met and worked with a number of Chief Information Officers (CIOs). So when I got to Folsom, California, and met Doug Busch, the (now former) CIO of Intel Corporation, I expected him to fit the mold that I had seen so many times before. Doug was nothing like I expected. His first words during the interview were, "One of the things I reflect on is that I am totally unqualified for this job. I was brought into technology sideways." Doug doesn't even look like your typical corporate executive. Despite his title, I qualify him as an ordinary guy. Although certainly professional, he has a full gray beard and is very casual and down-to-earth in his mannerisms. He laughed often and seemed intently interested in our conversation, in spite of the fact that he was busy preparing for a major leadership conference.

While we sat in the Intel cafeteria, Doug told me about a series of twists and turns in his life. He seemed very happy with the result so far. "When I came out of high school, I wanted to be the next Linus Pauling and win a Nobel Prize. I went to college to study biology. But after a couple of years it became clear that biology was not for me. So I dropped out of college, bought an old van, left Ohio for the West Coast, and picked fruit along the way as part of a United States Department of Agriculture program. It was an extremely lame old van and the engine blew when I got to Santa Rosa, California. I literally had no money, no friends in town, no transport, and nowhere to live. I met a man who gave me a job on a second shift clean-up crew in a poultry factory—not very glamorous. But the experience I got working in the plant, combined with my experience of fixing the van, taught me that I liked working on mechanical stuff. So I went to engineering school and eventually ended up at Intel. The point is, I was faced with no money, no place to live, and no job. And everything turned out fine. So throughout my career, I have always felt, screw it, if they fire me, I can be an auto mechanic. Ever since my fruit-picking days, I am very comfortable taking risks knowing that everything always works out fine."

Doug claimed, "The best things I have ever done in my career came shortly after I decided that the best thing that could happen to me is that they would fire me. As long as you are sitting there saying to yourself, 'Shoot, if I do this I might get a bad review,' or 'I might not get a promotion,' or 'Someone might fire me,' you are never going to take the risk. Instead, go and do what you want to do because you think there is value in it. Not for personal reasons, but because you believe it is the right thing to do for the mission of the organization. For me, whenever I took those risks, everything was neutral or positive in the end. Some of them did not pay off, but I never got beat up. In some cases they turned out to be big wins."

Fear of failure prevents action. Without action there is no progress. In life there are no failures, only chances to learn and grow. If you never worry about getting lost, you will always be on the right path. If you're always scanning your current environment for things you can learn, for people who can help, and resources you can use, you'll always be finding them and never feel lost. This path can lead to great places, as Doug Busch taught me. Even the most successful people often come from the most humble roots.

Making It Happen

There's always uncertainty in making a decision but when you recognize that there's opportunity on every path, you can trust that you are never lost and are not making mistakes. To take that first leap of faith, start asking yourself simple questions about your current situation. Use the following questions and concepts to affirm where you are and use the answers to take action.

COMMIT TO YOUR PATH

Remind yourself that it doesn't really matter which path you go down. Just choose. Avoid thinking of decisions as long-term semi-permanent choices. If your life is designed with many paths, you can change direction anytime you want. With the right mind-set, you are never lost. Every detour provides a new experience. How do you feel about where you are today? Are you engaged and playing full out, or do you feel tired and drained at the end of the day? If the latter, it may be an indication that you are not committed to your chosen path. Look for, and list out, all of the reasons why the path you are on is the right one. What can you learn from where you are going and where you have been? Remember, there is no right or wrong path. Just choose and commit.

COMMIT TO YOUR HAPPINESS

Although there are no wrong paths, do not use this concept as an excuse to remain dissatisfied or unsuccessful. Sometimes you need to change direction. If you can't commit to your path, then reshift your focus to commit to something else that will make you happy. Sometimes this means leaving a secure, yet unsatisfying job, or ending a steady but dysfunctional relationship. Move on from the things that make you play small or keep you in a rut. Ironically, many times we fear losing something that we don't even have. We let fear of failure prevent action. The things that don't turn out as expected are often the greatest learning opportunities.

OVERCOME DECIDOPHOBIA

Most people suffer from a mild form of "decidophobia," the fear of making decisions. But in life there are no right decisions or wrong decisions. There are only decisions. And once you make a decision, avoid rethinking it. Although you want to learn from the past, don't question the wisdom of your decision. Don't look back, or you might turn into a pillar of salt. Remember, what you focus on expands. If you believe you are on the right path, you will begin to see the opportunities and reasons why it was the right decision. Always move forward. Movement in any direction is better than stagnation or indecision.

LISTEN TO A SILENT MIND

Empty the clutter of your mind and listen to your inner voice. One useful technique is to write in a journal. Get a blank notebook and start writing. Start writing about anything. Write about what you know. Write about how you feel. Write whatever comes to mind. Keep writing. After a while, your writing will shift to subconscious topics—things hidden from your conscious mind—the silent mind.

In addition to journaling, listen to your body. Your body often tells you, subtly, if you are on the right path. Your thoughts change the way you hold your body. Check your breathing. Aspirations are about breathing life into something you love. You can't aspire when you aren't breathing properly.

SECRET #3

Remember That Opportunity Knocks Often, but Sometimes Softly

The reason why most people don't hear opportunity knock is that they are over at a friend's house pouring out a hard-luck story. And if they did hear opportunity knock, they'd complain about the noise.

—Anonymous

*I*n my creativity classes, I show a video developed by the University of Illinois to demonstrate an amazing capability of the brain. In this video there are six people wearing T-shirts. Three are wearing white T-shirts; three are wearing black T-shirts. Each team of three has a basketball. Before starting the video I tell the audience that this is a test of their ability to focus and pay attention to directions. Their task is to count the number of times that the team in the white T-shirts passes the ball to each other. I then play the 45-second video. When it is finished I ask the group how many times the ball was passed. Some people count 15. More count 16. Most count 17. The correct answer is 18. But that is not what is truly important. Because 95 percent of the people completely miss an extremely unusual event that happens during the video, I show the video a second time. This time I tell the audience not to count; just watch. About halfway through the video there is a huge gasp from the audience when a big hairy gorilla (actually a human in a gorilla suit) walks straight onto the basketball court, beats its chest, and walks off. Less than 5 percent of the audience saw this happen the first time. In fact, most people don't even believe I am showing them the same video the second time. It's a fascinating illustration of the power of and hazards of focus. (You can watch and purchase this video at http://viscog.beckman.uiuc.edu/grafs/demos/15.html.)

Remember the idea in Secret #2 that "what you focus on expands"? There's another part to this idea: What you focus on expands to the exclusion of everything else. The brain has an amazing ability to focus. The Reticular Activating System filters out 99.9 percent of what we see so that we aren't overwhelmed by stimuli. Each day we are inundated with information, so we learn to focus and block out stimuli by necessity. In this process, we miss major events, massive things that walk right in front of our noses—even if they present themselves as a big hairy gorilla. Think about it. When we are so focused on achieving our goals, we often miss big, life-changing opportunities. Yes, opportunity knocks often, sometimes softly, and more often than not, sometimes loudly. Opportunity could be screaming and yelling at us, and yet we ignore it.

People who live goal-free are constantly watching for new opportunities that present themselves in unexpected ways. With open minds—and open eyes—they're able to identify opportunities anywhere, even in unlikely places, and anytime, even in tragedy. They keep their minds clear of clutter to allow subtle messages to appear, because on the road of life you need to be on the lookout for hidden signposts.

Before You Open the Door, Look Inside

Sometimes the first place to look for hidden opportunities is within ourselves. While we have resources all around us, we can also look internally at our own skills and generate opportunities. We may not even realize that a particular skill we have is an opportunity, but that's the beauty of living goal-free. We open ourselves up to other skills that we might not have taken a second look at if we were focused on a particular goal.

In his last book, *Critical Path* (St. Martin's Press, 1981), Buckminster Fuller, inventor of the geodesic dome, provided some powerful words of wisdom. He wrote:

> *The things to do are: the things that need doing: that you see need to be done, and no one else seems to see the need to be done. Then you will conceive your own way of doing that which needs to be done—that no one else has told you to do or how to do it. This will bring out the real you that often gets buried inside a character that has acquired a superficial array of behaviors induced or imposed by others on the individual.*

What does this have to do with your unrecognized skill? Take a look around you and see what needs to be done. Notice what you are already doing. Chances are that you are already doing something that needs to be done using a skill you didn't even know you had. Some of the most amazing things in life appear when we address what seems obvious to us, yet no one else is doing anything about it.

One of the people I met during my travels is Danny Siegel, the founder of a charitable organization called Ziv Tzedakah. His story is a great example of doing what needs to be done and using a skill he already had and didn't even realize was valuable. I went to his apartment in Rockville, Maryland, and Danny greeted me at the door, looking somewhat frazzled. I quickly learned that frazzled was normal for Danny Siegel. As we spoke, he sat in his rocking chair playing with a rubber band, rocking back and forth. He would frequently get up and get books from his enormous library, and as he walked around the room he straightened the books, making sure they were evenly spaced and perfectly aligned. He'd then sit down and continue his rocking and rubber-band stretching. He was up and down at least 30 times in the hour we spent talking. Danny, a man in his mid-50s, suffers from hyperactivity, Attention Deficit Disorder, and dyslexia. Early in his career he found that he rarely held a regular job very long. As a kid, he had a learning disability and was a slow reader. This shocked me, given that his apartment is filled from floor to ceiling with books, all of which he says he has read.

His opportunity began on one of his trips to Israel. Before leaving on a trip to that country, it's customary for a traveler to wait for someone to give them $1. This would then be given to charity while overseas. This makes the trip a mission rather than a tourist visit, ensuring safe travels. Danny told me, "On my 9th or 10th trip in January 1975, instead of waiting for people to give me $1, I began to ask for money and wound up with $955 without really trying. When I got to Israel, I went in search of the right people and places to donate this money. I had no theory, no foresight or principles to guide me other than that the money should make a difference. I would ask friends, 'Who is doing good stuff, doing good?' From that point on it was easy, and distributing the money went very smoothly."

When Danny returned home, he sent a report (a whopping two pages, compared to the typical 40-page Ziv Annual Report) to those who had given him money. He thought nothing of the fact that he had asked for the money and distributed it to those in need. It just seemed like what needed to be done—to perform good deeds and to help others to do so. At the $12,000-plus mark, friends pointed out his natural ability and urged him to establish a non-profit organization. So in April 1981, Ziv Tzedakah Fund, Inc., was incorporated. *Ziv* means radiance and *Tzedakah* means charity. "Today we give away more than $500,000 a year, without any formal fundraising. It is just this simple—we mail our annual report in April and an update in November. Whatever funds come in we give away. Period."

Today Ziv funds a number of creative and unusual charitable organizations. Reading the annual report for Ziv is like reading a celebratory magazine of wonderful, inspirational stories. Danny keeps asking himself, "Why didn't any one do this before? It seems so obvious." Yet, what may seem obvious to you or me may not be obvious to do. It feels easy and natural for you. Ask yourself what needs to be done. There are things the world needs and there are skills that we don't recognize as special because they come so easily to us. Take a moment to write down quickly, without thinking, the things that you like to do. Later take a look at the list—what skills are you not valuing or using that you could be using more? Then see how you could use those skills. Sometimes the best ideas are generated within our own homes.

If There Is Trash Outside,
Turn It to Treasure

Look around you. One of the many opportunities that abound can become your life's calling—even in the most unlikely places. If we only focus on one direction, we don't see everything else that is around us at any place or at any time. Keeping ourselves open, we let go of judgments and see new opportunities. You never know where your life's calling is going to appear.

One case that made a real impact on me was that of Bea Salazar, a 50-something Hispanic woman who comes from a modest background. I met her in a low-income housing complex in the suburbs of Dallas, Texas. Thirty or more children were running around enjoying themselves. Nearly a dozen volunteers from a local church were strumming guitars, singing songs, and playing with the kids. All of this happiness is Bea's creation. It only came about because she was open to new opportunities.

Bea chose this course in life when one day, as she walked past an alley, she witnessed a young boy eating scraps from a Dumpster. She decided to talk to the young boy and find out more about him. It turned out that he was a "latchkey" kid, and she learned that in her neighborhood latchkey children often spent much of their days unsupervised and hungry.

A disabled mother of five, Bea began her mission to serve the needs of low-income children. It started with helping the kids with food. Then she realized that many were in need of new shoes, uniforms for school, school supplies, and transportation. All of these needs began adding up. The responsibilities and demands of her mission grew over the years, but Bea was steadfast in her dedication to her kids. She has worked non-stop and has never been paid for her efforts. She never expected to get paid. She started Bea's Kids and has supported the program on $20,000 per year. Everything is donated—the photocopiers, computers, books, chairs—and the money.

Her crusade against hunger, illiteracy, domestic strife, drugs, violence, gangs, as well as poverty, has grown through donations and a team of volunteers. Founded in 1990, Bea's Kids focuses primarily on academic success while providing an atmosphere of positive reinforcement, love, and care. By also addressing self-esteem, cultural, and family issues, successful results are being more readily achieved.

Bea's contribution to the community has been immeasurable. Who would have thought that a discarded peanut-butter-and-jelly sandwich could lead to someone's finding her calling? All of this happened because Bea kept her eyes open when opportunity knocked.

Ranya Kelly is another person who literally found her calling in a Dumpster. Seventeen years ago Ranya found 500 pairs of brand-new shoes in a local Dumpster. She was speechless and shocked. She thought to herself, "People should not be throwing out new shoes when so many people have none." So she did something about it, and she is now known as "The Shoe Lady of Denver." She and other volunteers gather unwanted, brand-new shoes from retailers and distribute them to people who need them.

Your calling can be found in the most unlikely places. Sometimes the most powerful opportunities appear when you are most outraged about a situation. This outrage can lead you down a path of charitable work, such as Bea and Ranya found. And sometimes it can lead you to a new business venture.

Turn Outrage to Opportunity

I met Tina Nocera in Montclair, New Jersey. She had launched an interesting business that evolved from her experiences—and her openness to new opportunities. Tina tells the story of a time she got a call from her son's teacher. Her son was only five years old. The teacher called and said, "Tina, we have a problem. Well, actually your son has a problem." Tina was obviously very concerned. What could her son be doing that necessitated the teacher calling her to discuss this matter? The teacher said, "Your son is not coloring within the lines." Tina was taken aback. Not coloring within the lines? What does that mean? It sounded like a serious problem. The teacher explained further, "When your son is given a coloring book, he does not stay in the lines with his crayons." Tina was shocked—actually outraged—at this teacher's clear lack of understanding of child development. What she began to realize is that although children do not come with baby manuals, maybe they should.

At the time, she was working in data warehousing (the storage and analysis of complex data such as customer buying patterns) at Toys R Us. After this encounter with her son's teacher, she wanted to find more information on parenting skills. She got the idea of marrying data warehousing with parenting. She started a parenting newsletter. This received an overwhelming response. She then invested in the creation of an online web site called parentalwisdom.com. Her philosophy is that parents have little time to read the 30,000 books or visit the 18 million web sites on parenting. It was like trying to take a drink of water from a fire hose; you could drown and still be left thirsty. So parentalwisdom.com provides parents with multiple and trusted expert answers to their questions about raising children. She believes that parents are the real experts because they know their own child best, and they simply need to see choices so they can choose what works for their child and the situation. As it says on her web site, "We all believe our children are unique, so how can 'one-size-fit-all' in terms of an expert's response? After all, if a one-size-fits-all solution couldn't work for pantyhose, why would it work for parenting?"

Think about what you feel most passionate about. What bothers you most in the world? In your community? In your life? What are you outraged about? Where is there a need that has yet to be filled? How can you blend your passions and skills in a unique way to create something valuable? When you identify your passions and emotions, you can use them as a filter to find opportunity in any situation.

Find Opportunity in Tragedy

Sometimes the greatest opportunities come out of real tragedy. But we have to be willing to see the opportunity and take action. During my travels to Dallas, Texas, I met the lovely Jackie Waldman. Her life seemed like what most would consider a fairy tale. She had a charming brick colonial home in a gated community, a great family, and a pet dachshund, Johnnie, who kept her company. In the past, she had a successful business that generated enormous wealth. Life was fantastic, until she was diagnosed with multiple sclerosis in 1991. This debilitating disease caused her excruciating physical and mental pain. She didn't want her family to suffer with her so she considered leaving them. She had reached one of the lowest points in her life when one day, while watching the movie *Schindler's List*, she had an idea. Maybe she could make a difference with other people who had the same disease. If she could save a few people as Oskar Schindler did, she decided, her life would be worth living. So she launched a series of books on "The Courage to Give." She now gives speeches around the country and has appeared on television. As crazy as it may sound, she truly believes that contracting MS was the best thing to happen to her. "I look at my life now, and the life I had, and I realize that I had been fooling myself all those years. I wasn't really happy, not happy like I am today. I was living someone else's idea of what life should be. Now that I am living life the way I want to, my days are filled with passion and vitality, in spite of a disease that robs me of my energy." I truly believe that Jackie's courage to give to others has given her the life she was meant to have. A life of her own design rather than one she acquired by default. For her, finding her compass came from experiencing a traumatic situation, which is a common method of discovering direction in life. When you lose your job, develop a serious illness, survive a life threatening situation, or experience trauma, you often reflect on your life and rethink the direction it is going.

Create Deliberate Accidents

Jackie's story is a great example of making the best out of what seems to be a sad situation. She rose above what could have been nothing more than pain and tragedy and created an extraordinary life—she made the most out of her tragedy. But that's her story. If you want to live the life you want now, don't wait for something tragic to happen before you get motivated.

Even with an aspiration, many people are unwilling to change their lives to move in a better direction. Instead of taking action and making a decision, they wait until some external event or tragedy forces them to do so. John O'Neil, the President of the Center for Leadership Renewal, and I discussed this quandary while in his San Francisco office overlooking the Presidio near the Golden Gate Bridge. John's perspective is that one's biggest enemy is fear. "If I let go of the known, I'll fall into an abyss, I will never recover, and I'll just die. If I give up this crappy job that is giving me ulcers, causing back trouble, and leaving me miserable, what's going to happen? Most people fear that they'll go away; they won't be anyone anymore. So they wait until the heart attack tells them that they have to get a new life. Or they wait until they get fired. We remain in unhappy situations believing we can keep things going, expecting and waiting for something to happen—some intervention—that will either bring us up or bring us down. We always hope the intervention will be one that brings us up, such as a pay raise, a promotion, or winning the lottery, but often we expect the worst—something that will bring us down—so we tend to encounter more negative events." Fear of failure is a factor in just about everything we do. When people who are involved in something oppressive (e.g., an unsatisfying job, an unhappy relationship) for long periods of time finally let go, they have an amazing burst of creativity. It's stunning.

Thus, if you want to live your aspiration, create deliberate accidents, figuratively speaking. What I'm suggesting is that you let go of your goals, let go of the rules, and see what opportunities pop up for you.

I learned this important lesson for the first time when I was in kindergarten. We were given a homework assignment: to color in a picture of a tree with leaves. I was never, and still am not, artistically inclined. But that didn't matter. I wanted to do a good job. So when I got home I broke out my crayons and was getting ready to get to work when my mother saw me. Since she was an artist and interior decorator by trade, she was an expert on these matters. I asked her what color I should make the leaves. She asked me, "What color do you want them to be?" I thought about it and said, "Purple, pink, and blue." Looking a bit perplexed, she asked, "And what color are leaves normally?" I was a smart five-year-old, so of course my answer was "green during the summer and red and brown during autumn." She said, "Great. What colors are you going to make your leaves? Remember, you are the artist and you can do anything you want." After a few seconds of thought, I replied, "Purple, pink, and blue." I then feverishly colored with my crayons, creating a surreal masterpiece with bright multicolored leaves—never once staying within the lines. The next day I showed my drawing to the teacher. She stared at it with a confused look and remarked, "Stephen, what did you do? These aren't the colors of leaves." I quipped back, "My mother said that I am the artist and I can do whatever I want." My teacher was so impressed by my response that she gave me a gold star that I proudly wore all day. I created my own deliberate accident, straying from the rules, and was the artist of my drawing back at that early age. And I now have become the artist of my own life. That's what we all need to do: Create deliberate accidents to become the artist of our own lives. Color outside the lines. Use bright, unique, or nontraditional colors. Don't do what everyone else thinks you should do.

Dig deep and find your own unique gifts and interests. And from there, create your own opportunities.

Stay Connected by Disconnecting

Every day we are presented with numerous opportunities, but they often pass us by without our even noticing. In order to find these hidden opportunities, you must be sensitive to the environment around you. Sometimes this means disconnecting to stay connected.

Technology can be a wonderful boon to humankind, but sometimes we abuse it in ways that prevent us from really participating in life. For example, I have a BlackBerry phone. My original thinking was that this would free me from my computer and allow me to stay connected. Yes, it does allow me to stay connected electronically, but it also makes me disconnected from what I should really be doing—being present.

I once was having lunch with a colleague. Although my BlackBerry was sitting on the table with the ringer off, based on the color of a flashing LED I could tell if I had any new e-mails. I was waiting for an important message, so I was constantly glancing at the flashing light to see if it turned red. I received an e-mail every few minutes from someone—either a real person or spam. I did not receive the e-mail I was so eager to get until hours later. In the meantime I was completely detached from the person I was having lunch with, missing an opportunity to really be connected. This is how staying connected can interfere with being connected.

You not only miss out on real connection, but some of the best ideas and opportunities pop up when you least expect them. If your ears are plugged with your iPod and your eyes are glued to your BlackBerry, how can you really connect with your environment and other people?

An important point to keep in mind is, wherever you are, look at the situation from the lens of how you might discover a new opportunity. Most of the time we are completely unaware of the environment around us. We keep ourselves busy, and in the process we miss the simplest experiences that can have the most profound impact on our lives. The next time you are riding the train, instead of having your head in a book, look outside at the passing landscape. When driving to work, drive a different way—without talking on your cell phone—so that you will see new things. Instead of answering e-mails while on the phone, take a moment to really listen to what the other person is saying. You never know what you will hear.

Making It Happen

There is no prescription or methodology for finding hidden opportunities. There are just opportunities. When you let go of a focus on your goals, your peripheral vision expands to see the opportunities that surround you—inside and out. You assume that anything and everything is an opportunity and that anything and everything is possible. To help you crack open the door when opportunity knocks, try the following techniques and ask yourself the following questions.

FINDING HIDDEN OPPORTUNITIES

Sometimes the best opportunities are right in front of us. We just miss them because we are too busy doing other "important" things. What or who in your immediate surrounding can be the next big idea for you? How could a local store, restaurant, or friend be the stimulus for creating a new opportunity? The next time you are wandering around your neighborhood, look for hidden opportunities. Too often we miss the big hairy gorilla right in front of us because we are too busy or focused on our goals.

BEFORE YOU OPEN THE DOOR, LOOK INSIDE

Sometimes the best opportunities lay dormant inside you. They are in the form of a hidden and untapped talent you have. What comes easily to you and seems natural? Maybe this is a new opportunity. Something you don't even recognize. Ask others about your strengths. What do they see that you do well? You may be surprised by what they say. Secret #1, Use a Compass, Not a Map, discussed *acquiring* skills to help you move forward with your passion. This is a different twist. This is about finding a skill you *already have* and using that to generate a new aspiration. Something that comes with ease. Often these endeavors produce the greatest results with the least amount of effort.

LOOK FOR OPPORTUNITY EVERYWHERE

Keep your eyes open, looking for new opportunities around you. Let go of judgments. Opportunity is everywhere. What is the most unlikely place to find your calling? What bothers you about the world? What shocks and outrages you? What would you do with your life if you lost your health? What would you do tomorrow if you lost your job? Create deliberate accidents. If you want to live life now, do not wait for something tragic to happen in order to get motivated. Let go of your goals and rules and see what emerges. Color outside of the lines. Be the artist of your own life. Create your own opportunities, now.

STAY CONNECTED BY DISCONNECTING

Be present in the world around you. If you are now in a public area, stop reading this book for the next 30 minutes. Be completely aware of everything around you. While driving, turn off the radio and look around. Unplug your iPod, turn off your cell phone, and be part of the environment and people around you. There is opportunity everywhere. We are just so busy killing time that we miss it.

SECRET #4

Want What You Have

To be alive, to be able to see, to walk . . . it's all a miracle.
I have adopted the technique of living life from miracle
to miracle.

—*Arthur Rubinstein, pianist*

*I*n the book *Eleven Minutes*, by Paulo Coelho (HarperCollins, 2004), the main character is a prostitute who makes the following observation:

> *Of course, everyone spoke ill of her profession, but, basically, it was all a question of selling her time, like everyone else. Doing things she didn't want to do, like everyone else. Putting up with horrible people, like everyone else. Handing over her precious body and her precious soul in the name of a future that never arrived, like everyone else. Saying that she still didn't have enough, like everyone else. Waiting just a bit longer, like everyone else. Waiting so that she could earn just a little bit more, postponing the realization of her dreams; she was too busy right now, she had great opportunities ahead of her, loyal clients who were waiting for her . . .*

I only use the prostitute's story as an analogy for a common predicament. Many people are willing to sacrifice today for something better in the future. While the prostitute *may* not have a choice, many of us do. We end up doing things we would rather not do. We work in jobs we don't like. We surround ourselves with people we would not normally choose to be with. We are not satisfied with what we have now, thinking that something better will come later. Without action, this longing for more is never satisfied. Rather than appreciate what we have right now or what we've achieved right now, we bank on the belief that the future will be better. We have convinced ourselves that the achievement of our goal is what will bring us happiness, yet that better future rarely arrives. Even if a goal is achieved, it often does not feed the soul. Therefore, the longing for more continues.

The challenge is to want what you have. Only when you have a deep appreciation for where you are today can you truly begin to dream about what is possible. Your goals are no longer driven by an insatiable desire for more. The future is not a place to get to. It serves as a context for igniting passion now. We're usually too busy to dream. We get stuck in a rut driven by ill-conceived goals. We are waiting so that we can earn just a little bit more, or find that right time, thereby postponing the realization of our dreams.

Measure Life by Your Own Yardstick

When I ask people how happy they are with their lives on a scale of 1 to 10, most people say 7 or 8. Although this may sound like a reasonably high level of happiness, when asked to describe what a 5 out of 10 looks like, it is often compared to deep depression. Therefore, a 7 or 8 is only a small step from a life of misery. Regardless of where you are and how you define your scale, what would it take to get your life to a 9 or 9.5 instantly? The answer can be found in one simple word: appreciation.

We live in a society where we have convinced ourselves we need more. Life won't be complete until I have that plasma screen. I will be happy when I get a new car. I will be happy when I can afford a larger house. It's only been in recent times that many of these things even existed. The car was not popular until the early 1900s when Henry Ford produced the Model T. Television did not become popular until the 1950s. The computer, the Internet, broadband, and cell phones are all very new phenomena. Were people unhappy before these items were available? Of course not. Are we happier now that we have all of these inventions? Doubtful.

When we compare ourselves to others we create dissatisfaction. One of the most powerful elements to keep in your life is appreciation. A wise boss of mine once taught me this lesson. He told me never to concern myself about my colleagues' salaries. "When you get your paycheck," he advised, "do not compare your salary to that of others. Instead, ask yourself if you're getting reasonable compensation for the work you have done. When you compare your situation to that of others, it will only create dissatisfaction for everyone." I later realized this principle holds true for life in general. Look for the great things in your life rather than the negatives. Don't worry about what others have. Focus on what you have. Focus on the wonderful things in your life now, rather than what you think you want to have in the future.

One of my rituals is to wake up each morning and take a mental stock of how incredible my life is. I am always amazed when I do this because I discover that many truly wonderful experiences have happened to me. This sets the stage for the rest of my day. Instead of wanting more, I truly feel as though anything else is icing on the cake. No matter who you are or what has happened to you, you should be able to find pleasure in the simplest experiences. Take a walk along the beach on a sunny day. Savor the meal you're eating, whether it's grilled cheese or grilled salmon (try eating blindfolded without speaking—it heightens your sense of taste). Be inspired by your friends and family. Take a relaxing bath and reflect on life. Fly a kite. Smell a flower. You can be deeply grateful for so many things.

Appreciate, Regardless of the Circumstances

People often say to me, "Stephen, it's easy for you to want what you have because you have so much." Yes, I am fortunate to not be in debt, to have a loving family, to have a wonderful career, and to have good health. Although it may be easier for me than many others, I have met some profound people over the years who are able to appreciate where they are regardless of their circumstances.

I remember the summer when I was 19 years old. During my break from college, I worked in a warehouse in the maintenance department. The work was back-breaking. We would tear down cinderblock walls, put up new offices, move boxes and furniture, and bake in the sun while pulling up weeds by hand. I was young and in reasonably good shape. But I was so exhausted every day after work that I had no social life. I would go home, crash on the sofa, watch TV, and go to sleep early. I was drained of every last ounce of energy. This experience made me appreciate my college education even more. It became clear that I would not want to live this type of life forever. More importantly, I learned that being happy with life is just a state of mind.

A man I worked with in the warehouse, Manny, was one of the happiest people I had ever met. Truly happy. We would talk during our lunch breaks and he would tell me how much he loved his life. I had a hard time believing him at first because Manny not only worked 40 hours a week at this job, but every day at 5 P.M. he went to another job for another 8 hours. On weekends he worked for a landscaping company. I was a strong 19-year-old and could barely muster the energy for 40 hours of work. Manny was in his 30s and worked 100 hours a week. I asked him how he could be so happy given his plight. "Plight?" he questioned. "I feel blessed. My family and I were in Puerto Rico and moved here many years ago. We love living here in the United States. I have a wonderful wife and three healthy children. What more could I want?" When you measure your life by your own yardstick, it's easier to appreciate what you have regardless of your circumstances. What may seem like an unfortunate circumstance is really an unfortunate state of mind. As long as you appreciate your life, then what you do is not as important as how you do.

Okay, you say, but what about when you're really in a rough spot? What about the times when it seems as though you have nothing? When everything seems to be going wrong.

No matter what your external situation is, you always have yourself, your attitude toward life, the value you create in your life, and the value you create for others. The ability to appreciate life is directly related to the meaning you attach to your life. A well-known example of this is the character George Bailey (played by Jimmy Stewart) in the movie *It's a Wonderful Life*. Apparently having lost it all, George is suicidal. But when the angel Clarence shows him the impact he has made on others, he realizes the value of his life and chooses to live.

The great inventor Buckminster Fuller was a real life George Bailey. In 1927, at the age of 32, "Bucky" stood on the shores of Lake Michigan, prepared to throw himself into the freezing waters. His first child had died. He was bankrupt, discredited, and jobless. He had a wife and newborn daughter and no way to support them. On the verge of suicide and reflecting on his experiences, he discovered that he had been happy, effective, and prosperous in direct relationship to the number of people in whose interest he was working at in any given moment. Maximum happiness, effectiveness, and prosperity, he reasoned, could only be achieved by working for ALL people, everywhere. Like a true scientist, he made the rest of his life an explicitly documented, public experiment designed to test this hypothesis. He called it "an experiment to discover what the little, penniless, unknown individual might be able to do effectively on behalf of all humanity." Over the next 54 years, he did very well indeed. During the course of his remarkable experiment he was awarded 25 U.S. patents, authored 28 books, received 47 honorary doctorates, and achieved much more (Source: www.bfi.org).

Another moving example of appreciation in light of adversity is a story that comes from Paula Kay (P.K.) Beville, Ph.D. When I pulled into a driveway in Atlanta, Georgia, to meet P.K. and her team from Second Wind Dreams, I was ready for something special, but I didn't know quite what. Second Wind Dreams, it turns out, is a non-profit organization that grants "dreams" to people in nursing homes. The dreams are vast and varied—from finding long-lost friends, to swimming with dolphins, to a trip to a favorite restaurant, or something as mundane as getting reading glasses. One of P.K.'s first dream recipients was Mae Bailey, who wowed CNN and most of the nation as her dream of riding all the rollercoasters at Six Flags Over Georgia came true. Although blind, in a wheelchair, and on dialysis, in her mind there was no reason why she couldn't enjoy a day at the amusement park she had visited many years before. With a huge yellow bow in her hair, and to the amazement of onlookers, she rode all seven rollercoasters in a row (one of the cameramen threw up after the third ride and opted out). "Oh my lands," was all she could say as she rode each one. She laughed and couldn't believe she was having so much fun and that her dream really had come true. According to the nursing home staff, Mae talked about that day for the rest of her life. She has since passed away but her dream lives on. She taught those around her about having fun in spite of infirmities. By dreaming the dream and being willing to ignore her circumstances, she showed how to bring out the kid in all of us who still dream but feel we are too old and grown up to act on our desires. Instead of focusing on what she didn't have, she focused on the great things in her life.

Appreciate Yourself

Sometimes, in order to appreciate what you have in life, you need first to appreciate who you are. Too often we want more in order to compensate for the holes we feel in our soul. We indulge in binge eating to fill a void. We drink to excess to deaden the pain. We get into relationships in order make ourselves feel complete. In the movie *Jerry Maguire*, Jerry's famous line to his girlfriend was, "You complete me." But what if you were already whole and didn't need completing?

One woman I met in my travels performed an unorthodox but interesting ritual: She "married" herself several years ago. The purpose was to continually remind her of her commitment to doing for herself what she would do for a spouse. She would love, make time for, and respect herself. Only after having this type of relationship with herself could she begin to have a similar relationship with a man.

About three years ago she bought herself a wedding ring. She wears the ring on her left ring finger, the one traditionally saved for wedding bands and engagement rings. Her ring is silver with a huge blue stone, and it is a great visual reminder of what she's doing. "It's just so bold and blue, and a huge stone. It's something different than I would normally get. I love it." From time to time she will buy some wine and toast herself, "for better or worse to unconditionally love myself."

She was recently in a relationship with a man whom she loved. Things were going well. Thoughts of the future were running through her head. Then suddenly and unexpectedly, he broke up with her. She was confused. She was saddened. Then she looked at her ring and remembering the commitment she had made to herself, she was able to move on more quickly than she had done in the past.

Take a moment to take stock of what you already have. Take time to appreciate yourself. Treat yourself with the dignity and respect you deserve. Then you will begin to appreciate everything you already have in your life.

Appreciate the Whole Spectrum

When you experience Goal-Free Living, you have an opportunity to appreciate a broad range of life's experiences. Imagine what your life would be like if you did experience all ends of life's spectrum, from struggle to success. It would certainly be more interesting and satisfying. You wouldn't be sitting around waiting for life to happen—you would be living your life, experiencing it fully. When you see a greater spectrum, it also tends to put things in your life into perspective. Unfortunately our focus is more myopic, and we tend to compare our situation to the more opulent ways of living, which only creates dissatisfaction—wanting something in the future rather than appreciating what we have.

Doug Busch, the former CIO from Intel, said that he learns a lot about himself from his time outside the office. "I love the outdoors. I used to be a backpacker. I don't do it much lately, but when I have time off, I go on trips to Canada and Alaska—I ski and I scuba dive. We have a cabin on Lake Tahoe where we take our boats and kayaks. At the most mundane level, I just enjoy the environment and physical activity and getting away from the structured environment of the city and the company. At a little deeper level, I used to hike the Grand Canyon two or three times a year. When I came back from the trip, I came back with a sense of perspective of what I am doing and the magnitude of the world we live in. It gives me the sense that turning in my status report late may not be the end of the universe as we know it. We have a tendency to blow out of proportion the consequences of the decisions we make or the failures that we have. Being outdoors and having some sense of the magnitude of the world puts that back in perspective. This also makes it easier to take risks and think creatively." If you think that every mistake you make is the end of the world, you will be loath to make any. When you realize, so what if it doesn't work out it doesn't work out—it makes it a little bit easier.

Doug continued by explaining, "One of the things I have always intentionally tried to hold on to is a desire for a broad spectrum of experiences. When I ask some people what they want to do on their time off, they have very constrained limitations surrounding the stuff they are willing to do. I have always enjoyed at one end of the spectrum going to an awards ceremony in a tuxedo at a big hotel. It's kind of cool. On the other end of the spectrum is sleeping in a sleeping bag in a puddle on a canoe trip. One of the values of having that range is that you can appreciate each end of the range because you have had experiences at the other end. You can't appreciate sleeping in your own bed until you have spent a night in a freezing cold sleeping bag in the rain. You have to have the contrast to get the full appreciation of what you are doing. By the same token, you can't appreciate a cold, wet sleeping bag until you have had to get up at 4 A.M. to catch a plane to give a speech. Then, the sleeping bag looks pretty good. This spectrum is part of my philosophy at work, mostly because I enjoy it, but also because I believe there is value in it from a leadership standpoint. At one end of the spectrum I am willing to sit with the CEO and have frank conversations about business strategy. At the other end of the spectrum, I will move boxes to clear out a cubicle for someone or sit and write code. I still drive people crazy when I get involved in diagnosing infrastructure problems. It's not because I am trying to micromanage. It's more that I am trying to stay in touch with every aspect of the work. It is also because I am not attached to status. What I do is no more important than anyone else. In fact, the person in customer service who picks up the phone and solves a customer's problem is probably more important than I am."

When you create contrasts in your life, from one end of the spectrum to the other, you create new experiences. You appreciate each task, each moment, each conversation, and you're able to experience a truly rich life.

Being True to Yourself with $187 in the Bank

This secret starts out about measuring life by your own yardstick. Sometimes that is hard to do when you are experiencing the less elegant side of the spectrum. However, a simple concept like measuring your life by your own measures goes a long way—even with only $187 in the bank.

Some time ago I was giving a speech on Goal-Free Living to 200 business executives in San Francisco. Afterwards, one of the attendees came up to me and said he was intrigued by the universality of the concept. He told me about a sports psychology consultant who had an unusual philosophy. The consultant believes

that goal-setting during training is detrimental to overall performance, especially when you are coming up through the ranks.
This ran counter to everything I knew about sports psychology, so
now it was my turn to be intrigued. His experience was clearly
aligned with my goal-free beliefs.

I was so interested that I tracked down Dr. Doug Gardner, a
former sports psychology consultant to the Boston Red Sox. We
spoke on a couple of occasions over the course of a few months.
The first time we spoke, we stuck to sports psychology. When we
spoke again, I recalled that he had said he was driven by passion
rather than money. He laughed loudly and said as proof, "I have
only $187 in the bank today but I am not worried."

Since creating his private consulting practice, he has only
been able to earn just enough to pay each month's bills. At the
end of the month, when he has a zero bank balance, he starts over
again. "Somehow I find it liberating," he says. "I have to create
something out of nothing, again."

Although Doug understands that most people want financial
security, he believes that he needs more. "When you work on
your own, you can see the impact you are making. You can see a
definite cause-and-effect relationship. You make a difference."
Rather than worry about how much money he has, Doug sees
how much of a difference he makes. He is focused on the quality
of his life rather than the quantity.

The crazy thing about sports, Doug says, is that you never
have time to savor your victory. As soon as you win, you are on to
the next game. You can't enjoy your victory because you have so
much work to do for the next week. "It kills you. It's what people
get caught up in. Wins and losses. Something I have learned from
sports is very simple. You are going to win and you are going to

lose. But you are not *always* going to win and you are not *always* going to lose."

I asked him how players keep themselves motivated when they lose a lot. In response, he told the story of a baseball player whose team lost a soul-destroying 110 games in one season. The player was in his fourth year in professional baseball and started the year hitting a .187 batting average (this is about as bad as it gets in pro ball). Yet by the end of the season he had achieved one of his best years, hitting .310 for the first time in his career. Doug says, "He showed me that he could perform his best on a day-to-day basis despite his environment, despite the negativity, despite the losing."

The story empowered Doug personally. "I thought, wow, this is the worst possible situation you could be in—men don't react well to losing—and yet he performed well, really well. It wasn't about the money or the goal. It was about doing his personal best. That's not just a professional athlete," says Doug. "That's a true professional—a person who despite what's going on around him can bring clarity to thought, have purpose of mind, and act on it."

In life people tend to obsess about winning. Even more so in sports. Unfortunately, when you focus on winning and losing, you are putting yourself in an either/or situation. "I'd rather give myself a chance to learn each day, rather than win," Doug says. "Success is not always measured in wins and losses but rather improvement." Measure yourself against yourself rather than against everyone else.

How does Doug cope with his current situation? "I laugh a lot," he says. "I find humor in having to make another $1,000 a month. I'm not worried about success. I have always believed I will be successful. I just make sure that each day I am doing something to move in that direction. That is what is really important to me. I don't worry about when it is going to happen."

The key is measuring your life by your own yardstick and appreciating the life you lead. "Most of all," Doug says, "don't become complacent. Always improve. This does not mean never being satisfied. It's a cliché when someone says they are never satisfied. They don't understand what they really mean. You must be satisfied with everything you've accomplished. At the same time, recognize that you can do more and better. You have to appreciate the struggle. I appreciate my struggle. I don't like the fact that I have $187 in the bank right now, but at the same time I do like it. It's really weird. I truly like it. I like it because it forces me to go out there and seek creative ways to do what I love to do without compromise. It gets me off my butt and out there playing. It forces me to be extremely creative, to not compromise. And it has given me the opportunity to spend more time with my daughter."

Doug concluded, "I'm not saying I am perfect. Of course I'm not. I'm the first to admit my biggest blunders and mistakes. I don't try and reflect perfection. I try and reflect humanism. I'm so fallible it's funny. And I'm a doctor! People spend too much time on the past and the future and don't focus on right here right now. You all have choices. Goals constrict your choices."

Making It Happen

In order to have the life you want now, you have to appreciate the life you have now. Unfortunately, we are always so busy chasing our goals that we are constantly working to get somewhere.

Rather than focus on our goals, wanting the next big thing, or waiting for that "better" future, enjoy the view now. Have a deep appreciation for where you are today. Only then can you truly begin to dream about the future.

MEASURE LIFE BY YOUR OWN YARDSTICK

On a scale from 1 to 10, how would you rate your life? If it's less than 10, then you need to stop, look at your life, and begin to appreciate what you have on your own standards and stop trying to live by the standards of others. For a moment, turn off your need to have more. Look at where you are. Do not compare yourself and your situation to that of others. Focus on what you have right now and not what you want to have in the future. To do this, wake up each morning and make note of how incredible your life is. No matter what your situation, you can appreciate where you are now. Make the list in your head, or write it on a piece of paper. Keep a gratitude journal. Keep the list in front of you as a reminder. Savor the moment. Be inspired. Be grateful.

APPRECIATE YOURSELF

To appreciate your life, you first have to appreciate yourself. You don't need anyone or anything to complete you. Give yourself the dignity and respect you deserve. Buy yourself something as a constant reminder of your commitment to yourself. Marry yourself. Appreciate yourself. Look at the positive impact you are making in the world.

Avoid making judgments. Success is not measured in wins and losses. Rather it is measured by improvement. Measure yourself against yourself and not against others. And when you do win, be sure to celebrate your victories.

APPRECIATE THE WHOLE SPECTRUM

Creating contrasts in your life can help you appreciate where you are right now. Do something you would not normally do. Sleep in a tent and sleeping bag. Volunteer for a charity. If you always drive to work, start taking the bus. If you prefer dining in upscale restaurants, eat at a greasy spoon diner. If you only eat at home, splurge and go somewhere really fancy one night. Swap jobs with someone for a week—someone with a less glamorous assignment. Vacation somewhere completely foreign to you. Experience the whole spectrum of life.

TRAVEL LIGHT

Instead of wanting what you have, consider having even less. Since 1999, when I moved to London, I have been able to fit everything I own into a few boxes. I rent furnished apartments on a month-to-month basis. By getting rid of the clutter in my life, I have found a greater appreciation for the things that truly matter. If I buy something new, I get rid of something old to maintain a balance. This way of traveling light has not only given me a deeper appreciation for life, it has also given me greater flexibility, the ability to change direction often and quickly. Although my lifestyle may be too radical for most people, the underlying principles of simple living can be applied by anyone in any situation. How can you travel more lightly?

SECRET #5

Seek Out Adventure

Creativity is just having enough dots to connect ... connect experiences and synthesize new things. The reason creative people are able to do that is that they've had more experiences or have thought more about their experiences than other people.

—*Steve Jobs, President, Apple Computer*

$\mathcal{D}$o you know someone who seems lucky? They tend to be in the right place at the right time. Things seem easy for them. Meanwhile, you feel as though the cards of fate have dealt you a bum hand. The world is organized against you, and you have to work hard to make things happen. The truth is, you can create your own luck. The odds of any two occurrences coming together are very likely; the odds of a particular thing happening are actually very low. From the perspective of Goal-Free Living, if you are open to any outcome, then you have a really good chance of good things happening.

For instance, imagine a room full of people mingling about. They are swapping stories of their lives, their accomplishments, and their dreams. You ask them to share one simple piece of data: the month and day of their birth. Each person goes up to the next, shakes hands, and says his birthday. In a matter of minutes, you will inevitably hear someone shout, "Oh my, we have the same birthday. What are the odds of that?" That is a very good question. What are the odds of two people in the same room having the same birthday? If you enjoy probability, you would know that you need 367 people to guarantee that two people in a room have the same birthday. There are 366 days in a leap year, so you need one person for each day, plus one. But it gets more interesting if you ask the question, "How many people do you need in a room to have a 50 percent chance that two people will have the same birthday?" Some people immediately assume it is half of 367, or roughly 184. That's a logical guess but incorrect. In fact, you need only 23 people in a room to have a 50 percent chance that two people will have the same birthday. Try it sometime and you will be shocked. With just 40 people you will have a nearly 90 percent chance that two people will have the same birthday.

How about a *particular* birthday? For example, my birthday is April 25. How many people would I need to have in a room to have a 50/50 chance that there is another person with *my* birthday? Surprisingly, the number now increases to over 600. So the likelihood of a *generalized* event happening is quite high. The likelihood of a *particular* event happening is quite low. When we set goals, we are looking for a *particular* event to occur. That is, we have defined a specific outcome we are looking to achieve. To make that happen requires a large number of things coming together in a particular way.

Contrast that with Goal-Free Living and the odds are much more in your favor. When you are not looking for a specific outcome, but instead are open to *any* outcome that could be of interest, the likelihood of a synchronistic event happening is very high.

Regardless of whether you are goal-oriented or goal-free, in order to make things happen, you need to collect experiences—

experiences that can be brought together to enable creative living. In order to live a creative life, we need to learn how to seek out adventure, try new things, gather new experiences. People who live extraordinary lives think like explorers. They know that diverse experiences enrich their view of the world. Every day offers a chance to explore and discover.

Creativity is one of the secret ingredients to Goal-Free Living. As Steve Jobs indicates, creativity is about collecting and connecting experiences. That is what this secret is about: seeking out adventure to collect new experiences so that connections can happen and create wonderful things in your life.

Reconnect with Your Childhood

You may think that as you get older you gather more experiences. The reality is, most of us repeat the same experiences over and over. Instead of 20 years of experience, we've had the same one year of experience 20 times.

For children, everything is a new experience. As children, we were passionate and creative; our minds filled with limitless possibilities and wonder. Numerous studies have shown that 98 percent of 5-year-old children are highly creative, while only 2 percent of adults are. How did we go from being creative, passionate, playful children to adults filled with burden, rigidity, and stress?

One obstacle is our diminished ability to *be* creative and to *live* creatively. A creative mind is a playful mind, one stirred by passion and possibility rather than deterred by fear and obligation—a mind that can develop new ideas and bring those ideas to fruition. As children we view the world with fresh eyes. Children are not focused—they are collecting dots. New experiences. It all changes once we start going to school. We are taught to memorize and regurgitate facts; to generate *particular* outcomes. Peer pressure sets in and we all feel compelled to wear the same brand of sneakers. We stop thinking for ourselves. As we get older, we continue through life planning every step—and eliminate dots. We go to college, we choose a major, and eventually get the best job we can. What do we have left? One dot. We know that dot— our area of expertise—really well but we have nothing else to connect it to. Instead of collecting new experiences, we become focused on one area. We no longer try new things. We continually choose the same path and use the same approaches for living life, neglecting to check whether they are producing the results we really want.

The way we have done things in the past is not necessarily the best way to do them in the future. Unfortunately, it can be difficult to get out of the rut and start seeking adventure. How can you reconnect with the creative outlook of a child? One of the people I met on the road shared a technique for doing just that: improv comedy. I met Doug Stevenson in the crowded lobby of Le Meridien Hotel in downtown Chicago. He started the conversation, "I just celebrated the 20th anniversary of my 30th birthday. And I have never felt more alive." However, when he was younger he had felt constrained to the straightjacket of his upbringing. It had been a struggle to break with that need to conform. "I graduated with honors in college and went to Kellogg School at Northwestern for my MBA. During those years as a serious, public-minded student with an orientation for success, it was drilled into me that it was my fundamental obligation to read the *Wall Street Journal*, the *New York Times*, and/or the *Washington Post* every day. Everything was goal-orientated, establishing goals in things that I was not entirely interested in. Then around the age of 30, I began to dream and discover my real self. At that time my father gave me a tape series from Mike Vance from Disney. When I first listened to the tape of this maniac talking 85 miles an hour—but with such enthusiasm and fervor about creativity—my immediate reaction was, 'I'm that guy!' Since then, I have been on a constant quest to learn more about creativity and to become more creative. I have discovered that creativity is about living a life that is self-actualized. It is the closest thing to being me. It is a manifestation of my highest self and is now the driving force behind my life."

Doug went on, "If I had one recommendation for people, it would be to take an improv class. The basic principles of creativity are right there. Improv gave me the courage to go with my ideas and to not worry about the specific consequences. Once I was writing a screenplay and was crippled with writer's block. My screen-writing teacher, Laurie Scheer, suggested that I write the worst possible screenplay. In doing so, it took the pressure off of trying to get it right. In improv comedy, there is no 'right' and there is no goal. It is just about play, much like children do. Another technique is to think of the worst idea and find some redeeming quality in it. You can find the lesson in everything. I'm working on something called *Brain Farts: How to be Stinking Brilliant*. We need to be better at turning bad ideas and bad situations into something good."

Creative living requires creative thinking. Unfortunately, sometimes we get caught up in the negative side of life. Maybe you're thinking right now, "Oh sure, improv comedy—I can't do that." Believe it or not, there are easy ways to get started. One of the simplest and most powerful improv comedy techniques is known as "Yes, and"—something children often do!

Children love to play. To them, everything is a game. One activity children everywhere partake in involves imagination and the phrase, "Yes, and. . . ." This interaction starts with one child concocting a scenario, such as making his fingers into a gun, pointing them at another child, and saying, "I'm zapping you with my laser beam." The next child then says, "Yes, and . . ." and builds on what the previous child said. The second child may say, "yes, and . . . I am wearing my mirror suit so that it bounces back at you." The game continues. This very simple game can go on for hours. Interestingly, if adults play this game, they are more likely to respond with "yeah, but" rather than "yes, and . . ." Instead of contributing, they have a difficult time suspending reality. If an adult holds his fingers in the shape of a gun, points them at his friend, and says, "I'm zapping you with my laser beam," the next adult would probably fall over and say, "I'm dead." Not much of a contribution, and the game would end quite quickly. Adults tend to see all of the reasons why things won't work. They put the "no" in innovation. To tap into your imagination, be a kid, and keep the play alive. Look at things with a fresh outlook. Put the "fun" in dysfunctional. This keeps possibility alive and makes you more adventurous.

Change Your Filter, Change Your Perspective

People tend to go through life as if they are wearing polarized sunglasses. These hypothetical lenses filter out much of the world, allowing only a small percentage of it to be seen. The filter is based on your past experiences, education, beliefs, interests, and everything that makes you, you. To change your perspective, change your filter. Unfortunately, it is difficult to recognize and identify hidden assumptions and beliefs because they are so deeply ingrained within us. It's hard to change our filter and see things with the fresh outlook of a child.

One of the easiest ways to adjust your filter is to stand in someone else's shoes. Cliché? Yes, but it's quite powerful. Try waking up each morning and imagining you're someone different. Make believe you're a detective, a mechanic, an artist, a gardener . . . it really doesn't matter, as long as it's someone other than you. You will then begin to notice things over the course of a day that you've never seen before—because what you focus on expands. By focusing on something different, you will begin to gain new experiences that you can use to bolster your creativity.

If you're Mozart one day, everything will be music to your ears. Your auditory senses will be sharpened. The birds, the jackhammers, and the honking automobiles will create a symphony in your mind. You will be much more aware of the sounds that envelop you. If you're Rembrandt, you'll see the world as art. You'll see shapes and patterns. You'll notice beauty and lighting revealed before your eyes.

When looking for creative ways of living your aspiration, use this role-playing technique. Ask yourself what Walt Disney, Bill Gates, or Steven Spielberg might do if he were in your shoes. It's a simple and fun yet powerful technique. Changing your filter, whether on a daily basis or just during one conversation, can have a profound impact on your view of the world.

Be an Adventurer

The best way to seek adventure is to be an adventurer. Sounds logical, right? Although it sounds like you'd be going on a safari, being an adventurer doesn't mean that you explore wild territories. It's really about exploring your world in a different way. To collect new experiences, you need to *try* new experiences.

Several years ago while speaking at a large corporate event, I met an amazing man, Jeff Salz. Since he was 17 years old, he has led explorations into the wildest corners of our planet—Patagonia, the Amazon, Outer Mongolia, Eastern Siberia, the Himalayas, the Andes. An explorer of uncharted territories, now a doctor of cultural anthropology who has a passion for studying the folklore, legends, and myths of current and ancient civilizations, Jeff knows how to face adversity with a sense of adventure.

I caught up with him at a coffee shop in Del Mar, California. While we were sitting there enjoying the sun on our faces, I asked him what makes him tick. What makes him different? His response was, "Some men see the world as it is. I see it out of focus." As a kid he lived in a magical world, and as an adult he has refused to leave it. He believes that is the key. "Most people learn to compromise. I live the cartoon version of the way the world might be. I live a charmed life. Although I am an adventurer and climb mountains that have killed many before me, I have never broken any bones. You can always find a way of operating beyond the ordinary if you try. The key is not getting dragged down by the ordinary. Don't take stuff seriously. I don't have much money. I'm always living life on the edge. But I feel incredibly successful. Wonderful work, good friends, and a family who loves me. I move through life with a fanatical degree of confidence and an unreasonable degree of security. I operate from the belief that there is no way I can fail. This erases all fear from my life. A great deal of unhappiness comes from living out the fearful aspect of one's nature. If you lived more fearlessly, you might take risks even if you knew you would fail."

I was surprised to learn that Jeff is the son of an accountant. Unusual roots for someone who has become a top adventurer: "As a kid I used to tell my parents that I was going to a Bar Mitzvah in Long Island. Instead I would go to Central Park in New York City, sleep in the park, and hang out with the bums, hookers, and cops. When I traveled out west, I once swiped a tray from a cafeteria in the National Park Headquarters, went to a glacier, sat on the tray, and scooted down the glacier at 30 to 40 miles an hour. I always try new things. I believe you need to leap before you look." What a great lesson for everyone.

For many, Jeff's adventures may seem a bit extreme. I am not proposing that you model your experiences around what he has done with his life. These may not be the adventures for you. Just try something new. When was the last time you drove a different route home from work? Ordered an exotic food that you had never heard of before? Struck up a conversation with the tollbooth attendant? Read a section of the paper that you would otherwise avoid? Tried a different brand of toothpaste? Ate dessert first? Start being more adventurous by changing little things first. Not only might they act as a catalyst for engaging in other more adventurous activities, but you may actually discover something more fulfilling than your tried and true ways. If you sometimes leap before you look, you may try some things that you have wanted to try in the past but were afraid to attempt.

Trying new things is one step but it is not the only step. Goal-Free Living also means being true to yourself, being sensitive to what you like, and having the courage to change direction when your gut tells you there must be more.

Seek Adventure . . . without a Safety Net

I was speaking at a conference in Singapore on Innovation in the Public Sector. Of the hundreds of people I met, there were a few individuals that really stuck out in my mind. In particular, one was another speaker, Michael Herman. Michael was tall, thin, and appeared to be quiet and somewhat shy. During our conversations he was quite soft-spoken and somewhat hard to hear over the loud clatter of the dining halls. What I initially perceived as shyness was in fact due to his internal peace. It quickly became apparent that Michael was simply calm and centered. All of the other speakers, myself included, were trying to impress each other with their knowledge and expertise. Not Michael. He listened and soaked in what others said. Then, at the right moment, he would say something that would be profound and insightful, without being condescending or arrogant.

I have stayed in touch with Michael over the years. I learned his whole story only recently while interviewing people for this book. Michael, like me, was a goalaholic earlier in life. This is not unusual. Many people need to live a life of goals before they can appreciate being goal-free. Unfortunately for many, they get stuck in the goal phase and cannot find a way out. Michael certainly found a way out.

Initially, Michael started out by following his goals. He received an undergraduate degree and an MBA from the University of Chicago. After graduation, he spent the next two years consulting, running financial spreadsheets for large hospitals, and helping organizations define and measure their financial goals.

Halfway through his tenure, he got involved with Outward Bound. In his spare time he worked with inner-city kids, building teams and community. He liked the ability to help others in such an urban-adventurous way. He then had the opportunity to go to a training program in Minnesota—an Outward Bound wilderness staff training seminar.

It was clear to others who were taking the training that Michael came to life during this experience. A friend of his asked, "So when are you going to quit your job?" Although Michael had not previously thought of that as a possibility, his mind started to move in that direction. He chose to stay at his company for another 11 months to complete a total of two years in consulting. The reason for waiting nearly another year? "I had a number of goals built into that date—pay off my car, reduce my debt, and gain some more credibility, just in case I would need it. I remember thinking at the time, this is the goal to end all goals!

"After I quit, I spent the summer leading wilderness expeditions for Outward Bound. When I came back to Chicago, I did not have a job or income and had no idea where I was going with my life. I thought that I might be interested in organizational transformation—helping companies reinvent themselves—but I had no background in it. My background in finance and health care administration wasn't going to help, and training classes would be insufficient. Besides, in my mind, I was too young to be selling transformation. Despite this, I still looked for ways in which I could apply my skills and interests to something that would appeal to organizations. I knew it would need to combine the bottom line results, finance, and critical thinking focus of business. I also wanted to weave in the adventure, the uncertainty, the not knowing, and learning your way into things from Outward Bound—the spiritual and the practical. I wasn't sure how it would unfold. But I trusted that everything would work out."

This limbo that Michael put himself in resulted in some interesting predicaments. People would ask him what he did for a living. His response was, "I make it up as I go." Not an answer that instilled confidence in others or in himself. At first he was admittedly a bit anxious. The dominant culture of the early 90s was one where his friends were quite wealthy. He would meet people whom he knew from business school. They were all successful, driving fancy cars, and in promising careers. Michael noted, "At age 29, I wasn't driving anything. Not a car. And I certainly wasn't driving a career. I had no credibility except for my business degree." What Michael did have was courage and instinct.

I asked Michael how he thinks life might have played out had he not tried new things, ventured into the Outward Bound experiences, and had the courage to quit his job. His response, "It's hard to tell at this point. But I can say that I am clear that the old path was not the real me." Michael was "jobless" from 1991 until six years later, when he considered getting a real job. A good friend of his, David, had a thriving investment banking boutique and offered Michael more than double his old salary with the promise of more in bonuses. This was the proverbial offer he could not refuse.

"When my first day arrived, I was still dragging my feet. I showed up more than an hour late. I knew something was off at a subconscious level. Had I really wanted to be there, I would have been eager, fired up, and on time. My first assignment was to clean up the 10-year projections for a big funding deal, already in process. I poked around the computer for perhaps half an hour, trying to understand the spreadsheets. I felt like a ghost. I understood all the numbers and formulas, but just didn't care about what they meant. So I swiveled around and just stared out of the window at Chicago's Monroe Street harbor. Another half an hour passed and I decided to come clean—with my friend and with myself." He never turned back to the spreadsheets. Instead, he went down the hall to find his friend—his soon to be ex-boss.

It was difficult for Michael to fight his emotions as he confessed to David. This was a turning point in his life. The fact was, Michael had always held this friendship and this very job opening in the back of his mind. It was his safety net, the place he'd always be welcome. As Michael put it, "This was my way back into things financial. The thing I would do if my adventuring all went wrong. It was good money and exactly what I was trained to be doing. And it was all dissolving because I just didn't care about the numbers, the deals, the money, or what it might buy. I was crashing through my safety net, sure that my career and my finances would be smashed to bits, but determined to save my heart, my soul and my integrity."

A couple of weeks later, Michael got a call from someone he had spoken with some months earlier. "She asked me to help her with a small research project. It was interesting and drew my attention. This led to a full-time six-month contract. Interestingly, I made more in those six months than I would have had I kept the investment banking job. I thought to myself, that's amazing. I walked away from the money and something that actually fed me showed up. It nurtured my soul and moved me in the direction I wanted to go. Along the way I have learned that when I want money—I ask for it. When I want time—I ask for it. I'm not asking anyone in particular. I have found that what I ask for shows up. Not like a goal. It's more like a space—an environment—that opens and I just ease my life into. It is not something I control, but it works.

"Everyone has the same purpose—just to be happy. When I worked hard to achieve a goal, to buy a certain thing, to run a four-hour marathon, to get through the MBA program—they never made me feel happy in the end. Or not for very long. I always ask myself, are the things I am doing to achieve these interim steps related to my happiness?"

After we finished, Michael reflected on our conversations and his life: "One of the side effects of living goal-free is that we don't end up with a neat and tidy set of accomplishments that define us. We end up with lots of strings that cross, weave, twist, and turn. They all lead to the current moment, right now. They lead out into the future too, but we can only guess at where they will cross again. Any thread can take me almost anywhere I need to go, but to sort it out logically in terms of goals and accomplishments can really squeeze the life out of the stories, the threads, this life."

Making It Happen

Are you ready to experience an adventure, collect new experiences, and connect the dots? Taking that first step is sometimes the hardest. To get you started, try the following techniques and ask yourself the following questions.

CREATE YOUR OWN LUCK

Anyone can be lucky. To create your own luck, collect many new experiences. Every experience is an opportunity for a new possibility to emerge. The more experiences, the greater your odds. Remain open to many different possibilities. This significantly increases your odds of making a good connection. The odds of any event happening are much greater than those of a particular event. Rather than waiting for luck to find you, go find it.

TAKE IMPROV COMEDY CLASSES

Improv comedy is a great way to increase your ability to be and live creatively. You will learn fun and powerful techniques, my favorite of which is "yes, and." This is an approach where you build on the ideas of others using the words, "Yes, and" while eliminating "Yeah, but" from your vocabulary. Practice doing this every day. Put a jar in your house or office. Any time you or someone else says, "Yeah, but," put a dollar in the jar to prevent anyone from voicing negative reactions to your (or their) ideas and aspirations. Use the money to take more improv training classes.

CHANGE YOUR FILTER,
CHANGE YOUR PERSPECTIVE

When you wake up tomorrow morning, make believe you are another person—an artist, a musician, or a doctor. It doesn't matter, as long as it is someone other than you. You will begin to see things over the course of the day that you never saw before. The next day be someone else. Really see the world through the other person's eyes. You will see things that have been hidden from your sight, because what you focus on expands.

BE AN ADVENTURER

Leap before you look. If you wait until it is safe, you will never make progress. Your safety net has you play small. Try new things. Collect experiences. Connect experiences. Travel. Try new hobbies. Think like an explorer. What is a daily routine that you do? How could you do it differently? Creatively? What is something you have always wanted to do but have never done? What are you afraid of doing—and then do it? Have courage. And have the courage to change direction when your gut tells you there must be more. Your compass setting is not a fixed destination.

CARRY A NOTEBOOK

As you seek out adventure, you will gain new experiences, insights, and thoughts about your passions and interests. Keep track of these ideas in a notebook or digital recorder that you carry with you everywhere. When inspiration strikes, you should be prepared to take notes and then take action.

SECRET #6

Become a People Magnet

A single conversation with a wise man is worth a month's study of books.

—*Chinese Proverb*

You can discover more about a person in an hour of play than in a year of conversation.

—*Plato*

*I*t was a cold winter's day in Boston, a Saturday, two weeks before Christmas. The sky was gray and overcast. I was feeling lazy. I had a busy week and now I just wanted to relax and sit on the sofa and watch television all day. I went to my computer and checked my calendar. There it was, staring me in the face, an invitation to a holiday party being thrown by a fraternity brother of mine in Stamford, Connecticut—a three-hour drive. The lazy part of my mind (and body) had decided it was not worth the trip: six hours of total travel time for maybe six hours of socializing. But for some reason, as strong as that part of my brain was at making up good excuses for why I shouldn't go, the other part was quietly suggesting I should. It would be a great chance to catch up with friends I hadn't seen in a while. I enjoy driving. Besides, during my cross-country trip for this book, I would drive much farther to spend only a few hours with a complete stranger. So I showered, got ready, and hit the road.

The three-hour trip passed quickly. Driving is always a good chance to clear my head. In what seemed like no time, I was at the front door of my friend's house. Wine in hand, I opened the door, and there were a dozen elementary-school-aged kids running around, screaming. In spite of the chaos, I ventured in and quickly sought out people I knew. There was one couple in particular with whom I shared a special bond. When I was living in London, Allen and his wife, Sharon, were stranded at Heathrow Airport on their way from Italy to New York City. It was September 11, 2001, and they ended up spending the next week with me. Since Sharon worked in the World Trade Center, it was clearly a traumatic time for her. The three of us went out a couple of evenings that week in September. It was a wonderful bonding experience. Seeing them at the party reminded me why I made the long drive: to make connections. And the connection that would have a bigger impact was yet to come.

As the evening progressed, a few of the adults were sitting around chatting. I started talking about Goal-Free Living. One woman whom I had not met overheard the conversation. It interested her. We began discussing it. We also started speaking about innovation and the work I do for corporations. She was an executive for one of the largest corporations in the world, and she needed someone to speak at an event devoted to innovation.

Although I didn't expect anything to materialize, over the course of the next few months it became clear that this company would be one of my largest clients. From a financial perspective, this was certainly a wonderful party to attend. But more importantly, the woman and I had similar interests in how we wanted to help the world. We have since become very close friends, creating many wonderful things together.

Making things happen in your life requires the help and support of others. Those with extraordinary lives learn how to meet new people, build relationships, and take responsibility for the next steps after a connection is made. When traveling the road of life, be sure to meet plenty of people. Share your aspirations with others and make specific requests. Keep your antennae up and look for opportunities to make new friends. Sometimes the most unlikely person can become the person who makes the biggest impact on your life.

This chapter is not intended to be a lesson in marketing or networking. There are so many excellent books dedicated entirely to that topic that I would never want to repeat those concepts here. This secret is about your intent in meeting people. Your mindset. It is about preparing for the conversation you might have with someone—the conversation that might lead you to who knows where?

Communicate Your Aspiration

Living goal-free requires that you have a sense of direction; something that wakes you up in the morning and gets you excited, something that has you wanting to play full out. Since anything of importance requires the help of other people, you need to be able to communicate your aspirations so that others can assist you in achieving them—again, not as a goal, but rather as something to play with. Something to engage others in. Something that gets them excited about your vision. When you are excited and can communicate that excitement, others get excited. You begin to create an epidemic; something that spreads from person to person, making things come to life in ways you had never imagined or predicted.

Your method of communicating doesn't need to be complex or elaborate. People often utilize an "elevator speech" to communicate complex ideas or plans briefly and effectively. Something 30 seconds long that could be used to convert people to your way of thinking during a ride in an elevator. That's useful. However, sometimes the answer can be a lot simpler than that.

When I was younger, everyone thought I was going to be a game show host. I used to watch the *Gong Show* and thought I would love to be the next Chuck Barris, front and center on the stage, improvising rather than acting. Having fun. That was certainly one of my childhood dreams. Like most dreams, the possibility of that happening faded as the years marched on. Then a few years ago the dream popped back into my head. I began to think that maybe I should revisit this idea. Since my life's aspiration has been to make a "massive and visible impact in the world," television would certainly be a good vehicle for making it happen.

Now, when people ask me what I do, my answer is, "Right now I am an author and a professional speaker, but someday I may have my own television show." They reply, "Really, that's great. What kind of show?" Of course I don't have an answer to that, because for me it is only a concept. So I answer, "I'm flexible. I have ideas for TV shows. It would be fun to be in front of the camera." Just because I said that to people, I had a TV show concept of mine pitched to the BBC, an audition for a TV show on a major network, and a producer worked with me on fleshing out a reality TV show concept I had developed. I hadn't actively done any work on my TV show idea. It certainly wasn't a goal because I wasn't doing anything focused to make it happen. But just through conversation I was able to learn more about the industry and get some inside opportunities. Do I have my own TV show yet? No. Or at least I don't at the time of writing this. Will I ever have my own TV show? I'm not sure. Do I love playing around with the idea? Absolutely. The goal-free approach to fulfilling aspirations sometimes can be as simple as one sentence to the right person at the right time. The thing is, you never know who that "right" person is. You have to assume everyone can help you fulfill your aspiration.

Assume Everyone Can Help You Fulfill Your Aspiration

You never know whom you might meet and where—and you never know what kind of impression you will make. If you approach each day as if everyone you come into contact with is an opportunity for a meaningful connection, you might just make that connection! As you collect experiences you connect with people who are one part of the path to your aspiration.

I met Mikki Williams in her apartment high above Lake Michigan in Chicago. The first thing I noticed upon walking into her place was that she collected lips. Lots of lips. This is a hobby she started more than 20 years ago, which has permeated her home and work, including a five-foot lip couch and assorted other lip accessories—from toilet seats to artwork. The next thing I noticed when walking into Mikki's place was Mikki. She had big hair. Really big hair. Mikki is someone who lives by the motto, Carpe diem! She joked, "I want to be thoroughly used up when I die. My ultimate goal will be realized when the check to the undertaker—bounces!"

Mikki's parents divorced when she was young and she grew up as the only child of a single mother. In spite of this, she retains fond memories of a wonderful childhood. "I aspired to being a good housewife and mother—to have the family I never had. If you want to talk about a goal, that was my goal. I practiced playing house more than most people. Maybe that's why I ended up being such a great cook and housekeeper."

Mikki went to Ithaca College on a drama scholarship, but when she got there she looked at the drama guys and at the phys-ed guys and immediately changed her major. "I was there to have fun," she acknowledges. While in college she met Gabe, a football player, whom she ended up marrying soon after graduation. She was getting closer to fulfilling her life-long goal when in 1969 she gave birth to her son, Jason. "Life was perfect. Gabe had a good job. We were saving for a home. I was pregnant with our second child in 1973 and we started looking at properties for our dream home. Then one night, I get a knock on the door. I would receive news that would change my life forever. Gabe was killed at age 29 in a car accident."

Mikki explained that she was the "typical wife." She didn't know where the bank was. She didn't know if there was any insurance. The next few months were hectic and complicated. She was pregnant, had a mortgage, little insurance, no job, and a 2-year-old to take care of. Friends would say to Mikki, "You used to be a professional dancer, why not dance?" Someone else would say, "You are a great cook, start a catering business." To make ends meet she eventually got into dancing, catering, and doing just about anything to survive. She started a jazz, tap, and ballet dance studio for adults. Then she started a catering business called The Happy Cooker. In total she started nearly a dozen businesses, ranging from a retail store and a health club to a natural health products company, all with great success.

Mikki had to get comfortable taking risks. "I like to say, 'Be outrageous, it's the only place that's not crowded.' That's the way I live my life. I dress outrageously and have crazy hair. But it's not that I try to be this way. This is who I am. I am just being me."

Her next venture was to take her experiences and ideas onto the public speaking circuit. But Mikki was not your typical speaker. She looked like Bette Midler and definitely stood out in a crowd. One day she received a call from a *Wall Street Journal* reporter who was doing an article on the speaking industry during the recession. "Why me?" she asked the journalist. "Because you stand out. You look different." Mikki was interviewed over the phone. A few months passed and she forgot about the article. "And then one morning there I was, my face, on the front page of the *Wall Street Journal*."

She was shocked and delighted and she decided to capitalize on it. She mailed the article with a cover note to a list of CEOs, and her marketing and networking savvy paid off. She ended up with a range of high-paying speaking engagements. One of particular interest came from a life insurance company in Johannesburg, South Africa. "I didn't want to go to South Africa just for one speech," she says, so for the next several months, whenever she was at a business gathering, she would look for people from

South Africa. "I am at a fitness convention and I see someone with a name badge—Sharon from Capetown—an aerobics instructor. I walk up and introduce myself. We became friendly and started writing each other back and forth via fax—this is before e-mail. A couple of months later I am giving another speech on networking in New York at an athletic club and I meet Kathy from Durban, South Africa. We have the same conversation, and end up faxing back and forth."

Both of these women were aerobic instructors, Mikki emphasizes. And this, she says, "is where people screw up in networking." They make judgments about what someone can do for them. As it turns out, Sharon from Capetown knew everyone. She was best friends with the people who were head of the Conservation Commissions, a group that oversees all game lodges in South Africa. Sharon asked, "How would you like to come and stay at a five-star game lodge. Just lecture to the locals there and you can stay for free in exchange for your speech." To Mikki this sounded like a pretty good deal.

Meanwhile, Kathy came through, scheduling Mikki to speak at the largest corporation in South Africa. Then Kathy asked if she would be interested in doing one last presentation while in South Africa. "I have arranged for you to speak on the great lawn of President Mandela's home. You are going to be hosted by the Premier and his wife. This will be the first-ever seminar after the end of apartheid. We have never had an American speaker." This was a speaker's dream gig of a lifetime.

As Mikki says, "Networking is a contact sport and I have been practicing since childhood. People seem to think that I have this unbelievable answer to all of my success. I didn't have an MBA, no silver spoon. But I'm a great networker and shameless promoter, and you can build any business on those two skills. Trust me, you can."

Mikki definitely has no problem approaching strangers. But what if you are shy. How do you start a conversation? How do you get things rolling? During my travels I discovered a simple way to meet people.

Start a Random Conversation

I was having coffee with a friend in a bookstore in London near bustling Oxford Street. We were discussing Goal-Free Living and some of the people I had interviewed during my travels. A curious look came over my friend's face and he said, "Tonight I am meeting with an interesting group of people. I have no idea if it will be of value for your book, but it might just make for an out-of-the-ordinary-story. Besides, since you aren't goal-oriented, every meeting is an opportunity to learn something new." Since I didn't have any plans that evening, 30 minutes later we were both on our way to Leicester Square. We wandered to the Equinox nightclub and stood under the giant neon "E." I was about to meet members of an unusual "dating" club. The club was comprised of nerdy, geeky, dorky guys who share techniques on how to meet and date women. After some initial conversation, we proceeded to a pub where we had some drinks and swapped stories. I started with a brief background on Goal-Free Living. I spoke of my travels, and of the people I met. I also discussed my technique of making believe you are someone else to change your focus (see Seek Out Adventure for details), and joked about how I was thinking of changing my name to a one-word name like Madonna or Prince. The name once selected for me by a group of creativity students was "Romero." And tonight seemed like a fitting occasion to don that name.

The conversation then moved from my book to the efforts of this group. One of the guys, Don, mentioned that he was taking a class on dating. I was of course curious, from a research perspective, to find out what he could learn in a class. If *these* guys are successful, then they must have found the secret to becoming people magnets. Don told me briefly about the class and the fact that he had a homework assignment to do: He said he needed to find something he was uncomfortable doing and do it twice that week. Of course I questioned him, "What are you uncomfortable doing?" He said, "I am comfortable approaching a group if they are all women. But if it is a mixed group, men and women, I am much less confident." I scanned the crowded and noisy pub to find him an opportunity to do his homework. There it was, a booth with three women on one side and three men on the other. I pointed to the booth and said, "There you go, a chance to do your homework."

He stood there looking at me, thought about it for a minute, and then walked to the booth. They all had blank looks for a few seconds. I thought, "Oh no, this does not look like it is going well." Then, all of a sudden, all six burst out laughing. They were smiling. I could see that they were talking to each other and to Don. They seemed fully engaged and interested. They laughed some more. Five minutes went by. Everyone seemed to be having a great time. Ten minutes passed. I was dying to know what they were talking about. After nearly 15 minutes I was desperate to hear their conversation. What magical spell had he cast on them? Finally, he walked back to our group. I wanted to know how he managed to get a mixed group so engaged. He turned to me and answered, "It was simple. I walked up to them and said, 'I am thinking of changing my name to Romero. What do you think?'" That was it? That's how he started the conversation? He continued, "They thought about it and said, 'No, you look more like a Bob.' The rest of the conversation evolved from there."

Meeting people on the road of life need not be complex and scary. And it certainly does not need to be planned, as evidenced by my new friend. You just need to get out there.

There are a number of ways to start a conversation, from the unique to the straightforward. If you want to talk with someone, notice something unusual about him: Is he wearing an interesting shirt? Is there some feature you can use to start up a conversation? Is he reading an interesting book?

Find Something Interesting about Someone Else

A few years ago, I sent my parents on a cruise of the Mediterranean and they loved it. When I was later asked to speak about creativity and Goal-Free Living on a cruise to the Caribbean, I brought my father as my guest. One sunny afternoon while the ship was at sea, my dad and I were standing on one of the decks, admiring the crashing waves as we looked down over the railing. Sitting near us was this middle-aged, heavy-set man, wearing a baseball cap, and chain smoking cigars. Not the type of person with whom I would normally strike up a random conversation, but my father saw that he was reading *The Da Vinci Code*, by Dan Brown. Before the cruise my father had not even heard of the book. Now he had noticed that everyone was reading it, so he, being a social person, struck up a conversation. He said, "I see that everyone is reading that book. Any good?" From there the conversation progressed. I introduced myself. The stranger in the baseball cap asked, "Stephen Shapiro, the speaker? The one who wrote *24/7 Innovation*? Everyone in my company is reading it." I was surprised. As it turned out, he was the director of a division of a major multinational corporation focused on the defense industry. He attended one of my on-ship speeches, and since then we have become friends, getting together for dinner and sharing insights about business and life. Something as small as a book can be the catalyst for a great conversation or a lifelong friendship.

Make Lasting Connections

Once you start making connections, it's important to make lasting ones. (More dots to connect!) So when you do make a connection with someone, be sure to follow up. The next steps are what matter most. This follow-up should not be a "goal." Rather it should follow your internal compass. How does this person fit into your vision and aspiration? What feels right? Follow-up can simply be letting them know that you'd like to stay in touch. This way, a call six months hence won't seem strange.

Toward the end of my travels, back in Boston, I met with Heath Row (yes, that is his real name), the founder and leader of *Fast Company* magazine's Company of Friends. It is a global network of business leaders, innovators, free agents, and socially conscious people who meet on the Internet and at discussion gatherings and workshops. We met in the magazine's office, a very dot-com-looking building with hardwood floors and exposed brick. I had not met Heath before, we'd only swapped e-mails, and I was surprised at how young he was.

Heath grew up in Wisconsin just outside of Madison. He was an overachiever and considered himself to be a bit of a dilettante. In high school he was an actor and played the alto sax. In college he was a DJ and edited for the school newspaper. He was also interested in anarchist organizations, grassroots media, and social movements. He started reading *Fast Company* at its inception in 1995 and joined the company as a writer in the summer of 1997. In October of that year he started the Company of Friends and it rapidly grew to thousands of members. His role is the "master connector."

"In junior high school," he recalls, "my teachers said that I was the only student who could talk to the stoners (those on drugs), the skaters, the athletes, and the scholars. I've always been someone who needs new ideas. I don't have ADD, but I need new influences. Maybe the reason I could so easily talk to so many people from diverse backgrounds is that I consciously sought new experiences. People have always said that the biggest ideas come from when you are jumping ponds. If you stay in your circle, you are going to limit yourself and eventually atrophy. If you jump somewhere else, that's where the connections are made and that is where the bigger ideas are developed. I have always been interested in doing that.

"I always need something new. My good working days are when I have learned something new, met a fascinating person, made an interesting connection between two disparate things, or shared something of value with others. Helping people does not

drive me. It is just a happy accident. If I can't share what I learn
with others, and it is only inside of me, it is worthless. Only when
you give stuff away do you get more back."

I asked Heath what had been the most important lesson he
had learned over the years. He said that his most profound learning moment came while interviewing John Perry Barlow (a re-
tired Wyoming cattle rancher, a former lyricist for the Grateful
Dead, and co-founder of the Electronic Frontier Foundation) for
Online Access magazine. "What he said has completely changed
my perspective and how I think. When John thinks about the
web, he doesn't think about it in terms of pages, he thinks of it in
terms of people. This interview took place back in 1995, the early
days of the web. John suggested that if you find a web site that is
interesting, don't bookmark it. E-mail the webmaster. He is the
one putting all of the knowledge together and knows more than
he is sharing. You do not want to read the page. You want to engage the person, the author. That conversation with John crystal-
lized things that I had been thinking. We all read books and
newspapers. But how many write to the authors we really like?
Rebecca Mead is a writer for *The New Yorker* and I will read anything she writes no matter how uninterested I think I am. It is always rewarding. How often do we go to the source and take that
extra step beyond where you initially connect? I have been lucky
to find myself at *Fast Company* because that is what we do. We
share the contact information of the people we write about. If
you read an article that you think is interesting, contact the guy
yourself and ask a follow-up question. You'll probably end up
having a very interesting conversation. It's about going beyond
the connection. Once a connection is made, what happens next

can make the most difference. If you read an issue of *Fast Company* that you think is interesting and after reading it you just put it down, we haven't done our job. The article should change the way you see the world, change your actions, and help you move forward in a new direction. It is all about what you, as the reader, do next."

Heath impressed me as a highly inquisitive person for whom networking isn't about business opportunities or social status. Rather it is about making new connections, gaining new experiences, and sharing passions. How often do you make friends with strangers? How often do you put yourself out there?

Making It Happen

Making things happen in life usually requires the help and support of others. Every moment, every conversation, is an opportunity to meet a life-changing person. And sometimes it is the most unlikely person who makes the biggest impact. Build relationships and be sure to take the next steps. You are responsible for making connections and moving conversations and relationships forward.

COMMUNICATE YOUR ASPIRATION

Share your aspiration with others by creating a short "teaser"—a brief statement about your aspiration that hooks them, yet leaves them wanting more. An example of a teaser is when the announcer says between television shows, "Next on Oprah, what the happiest people know for sure." This certainly piques people's interest. Create a teaser about your aspiration and then share it with others. Share it with everyone. Avoid making judgments about how someone might be able to help you. The person who will change your life is often the last person you think it will be.

START A RANDOM CONVERSATION

Start a conversation with a stranger by asking him, "What's the most interesting book you have read recently?" Or, "What are your hopes and dreams?" (It's easier to ask these sorts of questions if you've thought about your own answers to them.) These starters are certain to get the conversation rolling. They also give you an opportunity to test the teaser or elevator pitch you've created to explain your aspiration. Not sure what to say? Find something interesting about other people. Are they reading a book you can comment on? Are they wearing something you can relate to? You can find something interesting about anyone. If you are really shy, attract people to you. Carry something unusual. Wear a button or pin that is thought-provoking. Wear a button that says, "Ask me about Goal-Free Living." People will certainly stop and ask.

MAKE LASTING CONNECTIONS

When you read an article, book, or web site, don't just read the pages, engage the source. E-mail the author to start a dialogue. When someone shows interest in your aspiration, don't let the connection end with that conversation. Be sure to follow up. It is your responsibility to take the conversation to the next level. If you are interested in connecting with the people in this book, visit www.GoalFree.com. There you will find their e-mail addresses and/or their web sites. You never know which of these individuals will change your life.

SECRET #7

Embrace Your Limits

What you resist, persists.
—*Chinese proverb*

$\mathcal{A}$ former colleague of mine is one of the brightest people I have ever known. He is a recognized expert on information technology. He travels the world giving speeches and is the leader of a world-renowned research group. In spite of these successes, deep inside he has a belief that he is stupid. Although this is a powerful motivator for gaining new knowledge, such as his current pursuit of a doctorate, it also has a grip on him and creates stress in his life. He feels compelled to be the expert. He can never relax.

Another person I know has a strong need to be liked. She cannot do or say things that would have others think less of her. It's no surprise that she is liked by everyone. But she is always stressed inside. At work, she struggles with every PowerPoint slide to make sure it is perfect. Every conversation needs to be thought out in detail in advance. She has become a perfectionist, not because she wants to do a good job, but rather because she will do anything to avoid criticism. This is no way to live a passionate life.

And it is certainly no way to be effective. Think about how much time you waste trying to hide the real you.

We all have areas of our lives where we feel inadequate. Rather than fighting, avoiding, or denying these inadequacies, embrace them as a potential source of power. Don't offer compensation in exchange for your limits. This will only make your limitations more obvious and diminish who you are in the eyes of others. Instead, learn to acknowledge and embrace your inadequacies. Look at them as attributes rather than deficits. When you do, your inadequacies no longer control you; they connect you with the rest of us.

Uncover Your Inadequacies

Sometimes we don't want the world to know who we really are. Or maybe we try too hard to be the ideal person in the eyes of others. Hiding the truth from ourselves and others—and living our lives through the eyes of others—can be debilitating.

One person I met during my travels, Theresa, shared with me her struggle to embrace her limits: "I was driven by being liked. And it manifested itself as a compulsion to be perfect. In retrospect, I personally had no concept of what 'perfect' meant to me. I had only my beliefs of what others might define as the 'perfect person': how I should look, what car I should drive, how I should live, what job I should have, or who I should date. Viewing myself through the eyes of others was my sole source of self-worth. If people didn't like me, I would crumble. Yet if I had their approval, I would be high as a kite. If only one person out of a group of 200 had something bad to say, I would crash, and crash hard.

"To ensure that I maintained this perfect persona—at work or in my personal life—I would avoid taking responsibility for mistakes. I would either cover them up or try to make it appear as if someone else made the error. It's ugly, I know. But I couldn't let anyone know that I had made a mistake, that I wasn't perfect. And even worse, I never passed along credit. I would position situations in such a way that I would receive the praise. I must have been a horrible manager! I did all of this to gain respect at work. Funny though, how these actions were the very reasons I had lost so much of it. Oh, I was perfect all right—perfectly miserable." While speaking with her, it became apparent that she had somehow freed herself from this compulsion.

I asked her what caused the shift in her personality. How did she let go of her need to be perfect in the eyes of others? She told me, "It wasn't a conscious decision actually. It was more driven by circumstances. Because of my need to please all people, all of the time, I was dropping balls left and right. I was becoming irritable and burnt out and it was becoming increasingly apparent to my co-workers that I was far from perfect. I had to finally admit that I couldn't do it all.

"Then an interesting phenomenon occurred. As soon as I admitted to my shortcomings—those imperfections I tried so desperately to hide in an effort to gain respect and adoration—I could feel this tremendous weight lift. People responded differently to me. They did not react in the unfavorable means that I had anticipated—they actually treated me better, more sincerely. People wanted to help and support me. It wasn't until I showed the world I was imperfect that I started to gain the respect I had so longed for. I had this thought in my mind, from where it came I may never know, that I had to be perfect to be liked. It was such a deeply ingrained belief that I could not see beyond it. Now I have seen that those two ideas, being perfect and being liked, were mutually exclusive, and I have taken it upon myself to live more genuinely.

"In the past, I never allowed myself to feel any kind of negativity. You know, the power of positive thinking. Yet it was the denial of these feelings that caused insurmountable stress within me. Now, instead, I acknowledge how I really feel. If I am in a bad mood, I would say to the person I was talking with, 'hey, just so you know, I am in a horrible mood today and if I say something nasty, I want to I apologize in advance.' Once I embraced my negative thoughts or beliefs, I had permission to ask for help or to ask for forgiveness. But in most cases that thought just evaporated in the moment."

Before you can let the world know who you really are, *you* need to know who you really are. We often don't like to look at our own limitations. But if we find out what is underlying our behavior (or as a colleague calls it, "looking under your kimono"), we not only have a better understanding of ourselves but are then able to really be ourselves.

Bare Your Inadequacies to the World

As you may remember, during the Super Bowl half-time show in January 2004, Janet Jackson's breast was exposed to millions of viewers around the world. She later claimed that the incident was a result of a "wardrobe malfunction." It proved to be quite a scandal and for four months after the event she avoided the media. Then, in April 2004, she agreed to make a guest appearance on

Saturday Night Live. During her monologue, she showed the audience an old home movie. It supposedly showed her, as a very young child, playing in a wading pool. As she was splashing around in the water, her bikini top fell off. Janet coyly announced, "Oops, that must have been a bathing suit malfunction." The audience roared with laughter. That skit diffused much of the controversy surrounding her Super Bowl incident. If you poke fun at your own inadequacies, it takes the power away from others and makes you much more comfortable.

Mark Grossman, the film maker turned politician, turned publicist, turned menorah salesman (see Secret #1), is a mild controlled stutterer. For years this caused him embarrassment, so he would try to hide it. He did everything from word substitutions (using simpler words in place of words that made him stutter) to therapy and other training. He recalled to me, "After awhile I realized that my stuttering was here to stay and I should stop fighting it. I have since learned to accept and embrace this. I sometimes use it as an opportunity to connect with people. If I stumble on my words in conversation, instead of being embarrassed the way I used to, I now use self-effacing humor. It makes me more likable. I've found that I am still invited to talk on the radio even though I stammer once in a while. It is not a roadblock. In fact, it can be an opening. It provides me with a bridge to get somewhere. Think about it—a politician and a PR guy who stutters. That makes me interesting. Sort of like a basketball player who is very short. As a marketing person, I have recognized that this differentiation can be useful. Regardless, it is freeing to no longer be burdened with trying to hide something that was obvious to everyone anyway."

Mark's story reminds me of Winston Churchill, one of the greatest orators of the last century. He too stuttered and turned it to his advantage. His dramatic pauses and enunciation came about as he struggled to overcome the stutter. These pauses eventually became his trademark.

We all have something we want to hide. In the process of hiding, we play life small. We avoid and deny who we really are (mostly to ourselves). Embrace your humanness.

Make the Most of Your Inadequacies

When you come to terms with your inadequacies, you begin to find that you can use them as a source of power, a source of motivation. Often our inadequacies are fueled by emotions, so why not harness the power of our emotions and make the most of our inadequacies? They can even help us deliver our best performances.

Take some words of wisdom from Tim Davis, a former cab driver now based in Scottsdale, Arizona. We met up at Starbucks inside a Barnes & Noble bookstore. I spotted Tim immediately. He is 6'6" tall, with broad shoulders, and has a huge presence. After getting our coffee and exchanging small talk, Tim began to tell me of his transformation from taxi driver to comedian. "Most of my passengers seemed pretty miserable," he told me, "so I started telling jokes while driving. I liked to believe that the comedy would cheer them up. In fact, in the mid 1970s I became so good at it that I won a contest as New York City's funniest taxi driver. Then one night I picked up a couple on Park Avenue. They treated me like I was the lowest form of life in the world because of my chosen profession. I proceeded to drive them to the 21 Club, an exclusive restaurant. The guy got out and gave me a 15-cent tip. A 15-cent tip! I was so angry. I thought, now's the time I need to start doing something else. That night motivated me beyond my fear of making a go at comedy." He gave up taxi driving and became a full-time comedian.

Tim became so good that he got a call from *The Tonight Show*, when Johnny Carson was the host. "This was everything that I worked for. This was every comedian's dream. I was so nervous on the phone that I could not talk. I had stage fright and I was not even on stage."

For 13 years, this was the day he had been looking forward to, and suddenly he was tongue-tied. "I was gripped by the fear of failure." He never made it to Johnny Carson's stage. As a result of his "stage fright," he has devoted his life to studying the application of cognitive behavioral psychotherapy. He now teaches comedians and professional speakers how to give their best performance; how to inject energy into a presentation. His top tip? Recognize and embrace your inadequacies.

As he puts it, "Most business presentations, even though they sometimes have good content, can be very boring. As a result, I am not motivated to pay attention. In fact, listening to your presentation is on my to-do list, right after repainting my lawn mower. Therefore, you have to find a way of getting me to pay attention.

"To motivate people in your audience, you have to give them some passion. If you are going to give the same speech you have given in the past, just send it via e-mail. I'll read it when I get a chance. It is passion and creativity that make sparks fly."

How do you do this? Tim says, "You first need to trigger an emotion within yourself. In order to trigger your emotions, you need to trigger your inadequacies. Only when we feel inadequate do we get emotional. For instance, an overweight person doesn't get upset at a thin joke; he gets upset at a fat joke because he is feeling inadequate. So I needed to figure out what my inadequacies were in order to get in touch with the emotions that trigger my creativity and passion.

"Once you have identified your own inadequacies, trigger them when you go on stage. From this you will experience an intensity of emotion, enabling you to create a powerful reaction in yourself and increasing your persuasiveness. You cannot sell me something without this emotion. It's too boring for me."

As Tim says, "Save your emotions for when you need to be persuasive. Because, if it doesn't mean anything to you, it is not going to mean anything to me. And I'm going to go paint my lawnmower."

Recognize and acknowledge your inadequacies. Embrace and unconditionally accept them. Only then will they loosen the grip they have on your life. What are you fighting? Embrace who you are and share that with the world. Over time, you might even find that your inadequacies can be a source of power, helping you give the best performance of your life.

Tim shows us how embracing inadequacies can create a powerful presence by stirring powerful emotions. And sometimes your inadequacies can be the very thing that connects you with others.

Turn a Bad Performance into a Source of Power

As you begin to play full out, you will inevitably meet new people, take on more challenges, take bigger risks, and may even end up in the public eye. As you move boldly forward, even the most successful person can flounder at times. Especially if you are a perfectionist-overachiever, it can be disheartening to face setbacks and failures along the way. Sometimes you may even feel as though you want to crawl into a corner and hide. Instead, when faced with a potentially disastrous outcome of taking a huge risk, you can choose to embrace this experience as an opportunity to learn and transform it into a tremendous strength.

I know many professional speakers, coaches, trainers, and others who are in front of groups on a regular basis. Even the best of us have those off moments. During my travels I met Margarita Rozenfeld in Arlington, Virginia. She is a business coach, the leader of a networking organization for entrepreneurs, and a talented speaker. Margarita was recently given an opportunity to speak at a public event sponsored by a prestigious and well-connected business organization. She was asked to do a two-day seminar on building strong relationships. She felt greatly honored to be invited to speak there, not only because of the potential client opportunities that could result from this experience, but also because she'd be speaking to a group of well-known and respected fellow business leaders.

Margarita got to the meeting room early, confident and excited about her upcoming presentation. As attendees arrived and introduced themselves, she realized that there were two other organizational development professionals in the room. Although Margarita enthusiastically welcomed them to class, the two women quickly made it known that they viewed her as competition and were threatened by her presence on what they considered to be their turf. Although Margarita is not someone who is easily intimidated, she inadvertently succumbed to the pressure of addressing a partially prestigious and partially hostile audience. Her confidence and morale began to plummet—not the most powerful way to begin an important presentation.

To her horror, things only went downhill from there. What normally connected her with her audience—having the audience tell her what they wanted to learn—this time derailed the seminar into lengthy and irrelevant tangents she was not geared up to deal with. Being the consummate professional, Margarita's show went on, but she felt her energy and natural enthusiasm getting increasingly sapped as she completed the presentation. The self-defeating thoughts had taken over and she walked away feeling disappointed, drained, and deflated.

Margarita was not used to mediocre performances or their aftermath. Although evaluations were not as horrific as Margarita expected, her numbers were lower than she was used to or considered acceptable. She knew that if she did not blow away her audience with an amazing session on the second day, she would have missed a huge opportunity and may even have damaged her reputation. Her thoughts were bleak and heavy, making it difficult to get energized for an extraordinary comeback. How could she confidently face the same group who just witnessed her underperform?

Margarita called me soon after this first presentation. She said that her first impulse was to get up in front of the group and present the second workshop to the best of her ability without addressing what happened last time. She said, "This is only slightly higher on my list than running away to Mexico and not showing up at all." After being talked through the self-proclaimed fiasco and subsequent options, and ruling out the escape to Mexico, Margarita realized that this was the perfect opportunity to transform a weakness into a strength, a failure into triumph.

Her second class was about relationships (as in business relationships), including the importance of first impressions. Not every first impression accurately reflects the person who initially messes it up, as Margarita had just learned for herself. How could she use this seemingly negative experience to her advantage? This was the perfect opportunity to gain credibility and illustrate an invaluable point about relationships. Margarita walked away from our conversation energized and ready to put her creative mind to work in planning the next seminar.

She realized that if she were to make a powerful impact on the class, she had to embrace and acknowledge her mistake publicly—with confidence—and go on to deliver a stellar presentation. This felt like a risky approach but the only one that would be congruent with her values. She started off her second session—with confidence and a sense of humor back intact—as follows: "I want to thank you for returning to the second day of this workshop. Given my performance the other day, I expected some empty seats. I could have said that I was trying to illustrate my point about the importance of first impressions by demonstrating what NOT to do. I won't say that, but I do invite you to benefit from my experience, as well as ones you may have had in the past. As we have learned, even the best intentions and preparation don't always result in a perfect outcome. We are human, and sometimes our own inner critic sabotages the performance that we were born to deliver. Has this ever happened to you? What did you do and how did you recover?" This immediately warmed up her audience and opened the space for a meaningful conversation about relationships. Everyone has experienced failure and Margarita's courage and openness gave others permission to embrace and learn from their own mistakes.

The session concluded on a high note and she received the rave reviews she is accustomed to from the audience. Margarita's example illustrates how a seeming failure can be turned into a triumphant success with a little dose of courage and the willingness to embrace your mistakes. Each one of us can look at our foibles not as limitations, but rather as a source of power. Embrace who you are. This makes you endearing, genuine, and ultimately more successful.

Failure Leads to Success

As ironic as it may seem, people who work in customer service know that moments of failure are the best opportunities to demonstrate their strengths. One firm I am familiar with has a successful product that has proven to be virtually flawless. The defect rates are so low that customers rarely come complaining. In those rare instances when something does go wrong, the company really shines. The customer service team springs into action, going out of their way to make sure that the customer is completely satisfied. Customers who buy the product and never have a problem are happy customers. Customers who buy the product, have a problem, and then interact with the customer service department are customers for life. Someone once joked that they should intentionally have a certain number of products fail so that people could experience the customer service department. Failure sometimes can be an opportunity for even greater success.

When Dr. Doug Gardner, the sports psychology consultant, works with school sports teams, he encourages the players to focus on each play, not on whether they are winning or losing. He describes it this way: "With one high school baseball team I coach, after each game we go out to right field and talk about the game. Throughout the game I have trained them to never look at the scoreboard. Don't worry about the numbers. Just play your best. After every game we walk out to right field where the scoreboard is located, and I have them turn around and face it. I ask them, 'We won, today. Why?' or 'We lost today. Why?' The conversation is not just about the fact that we won or lost. But why? 'Why' is the critical question."

Doug continues, "I want to compete. I want to give myself a chance. If I lose, I want to look at why, without beating myself up. Sometimes you just lose. Sometimes you just win." After all, it's just a game. No matter what the outcome, there is always an opportunity for growth.

Mark Twain once said, "Twenty years from now you will be more disappointed by the things you didn't do than by the ones you did do. So throw off the bowlines. Sail away from the safe harbor. Catch the trade winds in your sails. Explore. Dream. Discover." He also said, "I've experienced a lot of terrible things in my life. Some of them have actually happened." The insight is that the world can look a lot more frightening than it really is if we allow it to. We need to venture out. We need to recognize that we will stumble. How we recover from those stumbles is what makes the difference between ordinary and extraordinary living.

Put Your Best Face Forward . . . Regardless of What It Looks Like

One night (during the writing of this book) I was giving a friend a piggy-back ride. I lost my balance and fell forward on the side-walk—with the weight of my friend on my head. Rather than my hands breaking my fall, my nose broke my fall—and my nose broke in the process. I had huge gashes across my entire face. A dozen stitches later, I looked like Frankenstein's ugly brother. Although it was not physically painful, it was emotionally disturbing. We may not want to admit it, but in our society, looks do matter. For a couple of months after the accident, when I looked in the mirror I didn't see me. I saw only bruises, gashes, stitches, dried blood, and open wounds.

A few days after the accident, I decided that I was well enough to venture out into the real world. I wandered down to a local nightclub. Rather than trying to hide my face, I walked in proud and confident. When people asked what happened, I would share with them the story. I definitely was not looking for sympathy. I wanted to be treated the way I had always been treated in the past. And I was. I realized that those bumps and bruises had not changed me in any substantial way. In fact they had freed me—freed me from a hidden (and sometimes unhealthy) vanity that used to drive me at a subconscious level. This doesn't mean I will no longer care about my looks. It only means that I am freed from the pressure of *having* to look good.

By recognizing and embracing your limits—those things you wish to hide—you can free yourself to be who you really are. When you do this, you realize that no matter what happens, no one can take away the real you. So, the next time you have a bad hair day, or have a huge zit on your face, don't hide. Hold your head up proudly. Face the world.

Making It Happen

Hiding the truth from ourselves and others—and living our lives through the eyes of others—can be debilitating. Uncover your underlying beliefs, and then analyze whether these beliefs are actually true. Very often, they are not. When we try to hide things we perceive as shortcomings about ourselves from other people, we lose our power. Often, we are so busy trying to hide our inadequacies that we end up not seeming real or authentic. Take time to acknowledge your own humanness and to turn it into a source of power.

EMBRACE YOUR LIMITS

What is your worst nightmare? What always hurts your feelings? What is your shadow side, the ugly truth you hide from others? Why does this have such a strong grip on you? What do you worry that people will think about you? What drives you to live the way you do? Why? Quite often the thing that drives us (e.g., to be liked, to be smart) is triggered by a hidden inadequacy. Rather than fighting these perceived inadequacies, embrace them. Use them as a source of power. Share your limits with others. Find ways in which your inadequacy can become a strength. Can it be a conversation starter? Can it differentiate you from others in a positive way?

FAILURE LEADS TO SUCCESS

Failures provide the best opportunities to demonstrate your strengths. When you acknowledge a failure and then take care of the impacted individuals, they will remember the recovery and not the failure. In fact, they will be able to relate to you better because of it. Every failure is an opportunity for even greater success. When reflecting on the past, don't focus on whether you failed or succeeded, won or lost, whether you were good or bad. Instead, ask yourself, "Why?" Why did you win? Why did you fail? Only through this reflection, and through embracing these situations, can you learn and grow.

DIFFERENT KNOWLEDGE RATHER THAN MORE KNOWLEDGE

In today's competitive world, it seems as though we always need to be the expert. But sometimes *different* knowledge is better than more knowledge. A colleague of mine was an elementary school teacher who wanted to move into corporate education. When interviewing, she was inevitably asked if she had any corporate experience. Her reply was always, "No. And that is exactly why you need to hire me." This bold statement earned her strong marks with her interviewers. She went on to explain that her noncorporate background provided a different—and valuable—perspective to the way the company had done things in the past. She was quickly hired. How can you take something that seems like a weakness and turn it into a strength? How can you provide a new perspective to an old problem? Where can you say, "This is exactly the reason you need me"?

SECRET #8

Remain Detached

The best things I have ever done in my career came shortly after I decided that the best thing that could happen to me is that they would fire me. Trying to be successful and achieve your goals is the surest way to be unsuccessful.

—*Doug Busch, former Chief Information Officer, Intel*

$\mathcal{W}$hile standing under the "E" of the neon Equinox nightclub sign in crowded Leicester Square, I gained some interesting advice from the London-based dating group I mentioned in Secret #6. I asked them what they felt was the most important technique for attracting a woman. They unanimously responded, "Don't try." One of the members continued, "When you are trying to impress a woman, the harder you try the less successful you will be. A focus on the outcome—the next date, a long-term relationship, or something else—is the surest way of failing. But when you are completely detached and are there in the moment enjoying her company, you have a much higher chance of getting another date. It makes you much more appealing and attractive to her. Besides, even if you are unsuccessful in continuing the relationship, at least you had a wonderful evening."

Detachment from the outcome is critical for Goal-Free Living. To be clear, it is not the same thing as indifference. When you are detached, you act with a commitment to the future while focusing on the present. It increases your pleasure today. It makes you more appealing to those around you. Surprisingly, it increases the odds of your achieving the desired outcome, no matter how big and bold.

This is the final attribute that distinguishes a goal from an aspiration. With a goal you really want a successful outcome. You want to achieve your goal. You are mentally and emotionally involved with the result. With an aspiration you are totally detached, living for the moment. You do not worry whether or not your aspirations are even achievable. In fact, you know that the biggest and boldest aspirations may never become reality. Perhaps ironically, when you are overly concerned about, and focused on, hitting your target, you are less likely to achieve your objective. Forcing life to go the way you want often leads to dissatisfaction and failure.

Anyone who plays golf knows that the surest way to hit a winning shot is to line your body and feet with the pin (the destination), and then focus only on the ball—as in the movie *Caddyshack*, when Chevy Chase says, "Be the ball." Focus 100 percent of your attention on the ball right in front of you, not on the pin. Because as soon as you lift your head and look where you want the ball to go, it is guaranteed to go somewhere else. Pros say this is the number one mistake made by golf rookies. It is the most common mistake made by Goal-Free Living rookies. Don't try to force life to turn out according to a plan. Allow life to unfold naturally. It will be a much richer experience than you could ever have imagined. As some say, go with the flow.

Detachment is a Mindset

At the basic level, detachment is really about letting go. It is important to note that detachment is distinctly different from stepping back and saying you don't care at all. It's a perspective shift. When you are less invested in the outcome but committed to the process, you can experience the power of detachment.

An illustration of this is the story of a consultant who was having difficulty growing his business. He was unable to close most deals and had only two months of work booked. One day he received a call from a company that was interested in using his services. Normally he would have been extremely eager, but they wanted him to commence the following week and he had a client commitment for the next eight weeks.

The potential client was clearly determined to use his services and so they offered him twice his normal rate. He was flattered but was still unavailable. The company offered again, suggesting he do a very small amount of work now, with the full-time work commencing in two months, still at the higher rate. He was amazed. This was by far his easiest sale. The more he told them he couldn't do the job, the more they wanted him. In the past, when he was "attached" to selling work, he was woefully unsuccessful. What he learned was that when he was truly "detached," he was much more desirable and was more likely to make the sale. When you try too hard, you are more likely to be unsuccessful. Now, before he goes to a sales call, he looks in the mirror and says, "I don't want this job, I don't want this job, I don't want this job." Since he started that practice, he has sold more work than ever because he has been detached from winning the work.

I have coached people who are looking for jobs and have given them similar advice. They were more relaxed in the interviews and were much more likely to receive job offers than those who were trying. People who are detached from fitting into a size 4 dress are more likely to lose weight, because they won't be overly discouraged by a lack of progress and can take pleasure in their eating habits. When you are detached from how your relationship will turn out, you are more likely to have a powerful relationship. You will seem less needy and more relaxed, making yourself more attractive to your partner. Besides, when you are detached, you can enjoy the process without worrying about the results.

The Difficulty of Detachment

Detachment may be fundamental to Goal-Free Living. But, as I have learned through personal experience, being detached is sometimes easier said than done. The more you try to detach, the more you may inadvertently attach.

Several years ago I was in a relationship with a woman who was beautiful, vivacious, and passionate. But there were issues. She was thinking of moving to another state, and this made me wonder if the relationship would last. Although I tried to just enjoy each day without worrying about the future, my insecurity about the situation made this nearly impossible. Instead, I ended up trying harder and harder to keep her, and in the process ended up smothering her; I came across as clingy and needy. The outcome? Not surprisingly, we are no longer dating. The more I tried to make things work, the less likely they were to work. Paradoxically, too much attachment to an outcome often yields a failure in achieving it.

Detachment is not always easy. Often there are areas of our lives where detachment is in fact quite difficult. For me it had been in new romantic relationships. For others it may be insecurity about money. For others it may be acceptance and being liked. In what area of your life do you feel insecure, are vested in the outcome, or feel the risks are too high? Unless you can change your perspective, these may be difficult areas in which to remain goal-free.

The Scarcity Fallacy

One reason we may have difficulty remaining detached is due to a subtle and subconscious scarcity mentality. We want something badly—sometimes being impulsive about it—because we are afraid that there may not be enough to go around.

We need to be more likable, because there is a limited supply of affection in the world. We need to make this relationship work because there is only one soul mate out there for me—and she is it. We need to work exceptionally hard because all of the jobs are being outsourced to India and China.

We feel that we must be successful in achieving our goal, otherwise we will have to do without. When you don't have enough money or when you believe you are financially insecure, you may be attached to earning wealth. Many times, this scarcity is just an illusion. Part of it may be programming from past experiences. My father comes from a childhood of abject poverty. He has a scarcity mentality about money. Making a good income and saving were critical. Years ago he told me that he would have signed a lifetime contract with his employer if they offered him

$150 a week. When in a scarcity mode, we are often willing to compromise.

The mind primarily seeks pleasure. It convinces you that you need to accomplish your goals, because achieving your goals will make you money, and money can buy you things, and things will make you happy. It's an illusion. It's the same illusion that plagues all of us as we grow older. When you are 10 years old, you convince yourself that life will be great when you are a teenager. Then you turn 13 and you can't wait until you are old enough to drive. When you are old enough to drive, you can't wait to leave home for college. Then when in college you can't wait to be old enough to drink. You are living for the next fix but never living a single moment you have. You keep hurrying through life, wanting and longing for what is next, believing that true happiness is around the corner. Then you hit your 40s, reflect back, and wish you were younger. Instead of a world of plenty, things begin to appear scarce. When we believe something is scarce, we think it has value, just as a diamond has value. The reality is, there are plenty of diamonds out there—their value is artificial and only based on what people are willing to pay. An abundance mentality makes detachment much easier. Therefore wanting what you have makes detachment easier.

Focus of the Mind

Another reason why detachment is difficult is an important survival mechanism. As mentioned previously, "what you focus on expands." When the brain filters most stimuli, it also expands what you are focused on. For example, when you buy a shiny new car, as soon as you drive it off the dealer's lot it will inevitably seem as though everyone else on the road is driving the same car, even though you hadn't noticed those vehicles before. How about when you or your partner got pregnant, or were trying unsuccessfully to become pregnant? Suddenly you notice everyone around you is either pregnant or pushing infants in baby carriages. What comes to the top of your mind is what you will see. And you will see it everywhere.

This is why it is difficult to quit any bad habit. When you say you want to quit smoking, the brain ignores the word "quit" and focuses on the word "smoking." That is all you can think about. Everything around you reminds you of the pleasures of smoking, causing you to crave one last cigarette. When dieting, our mind is focused on food. We feel deprived. We focus on what we can't have, and in the end our diets end with binge eating. I used to be a Coke addict. Actually a Diet Coke addict. There was a time when I would drink as much as five liters of diet cola a day. Every time I tried to stop, I would focus on it so much that I would end up drinking more.

How can we overcome all of these barriers to detachment? One way to detach yourself from something is to reattach yourself to something else. Something more empowering. Instead of reducing my cola consumption, I decided to let myself drink as much carbonated beverage as I wanted, as long as I drank at least two liters of water a day. It doesn't take much discipline to drink two liters of water. And by paying attention to my body and how much better I feel, it positively reinforces the new behavior and helps me detach from the old. Now I find I rarely drink much cola.

Although attaching yourself to something else is useful

when breaking bad habits, it is more useful during the pursuit of your aspirations. One simple way to start is to attach to the present moment.

Attach to the Present Moment

It is natural to want a future that is better than today. In our minds we create a picture of what tomorrow might look like. In the process, we become attached to these outcomes and start planning for that future. This myopic focus on where we are going makes us miss the present moment. Instead, let go of the outcome. Let go of your future plans. Attach to the intent to make things work now—whether in your job, your marriage, or your community.

A woman I met during my travels, Lisa, gave me a powerful illustration about how planning for the future can sometimes destroy the very thing you are striving for. A number of years ago, she was dating a wonderful guy that was definite husband material. He was attractive, successful, and fascinating. Sparks were flying. It was clear that he too was interested in a long-term future. "Right from the very start of the relationship, he began driving around neighborhoods showing me houses. In his not-so-subtle way, he was planning our future instead of getting to know me in the present. In his personal life, he kept putting off his present living in favor of the future. For ten years he lived in an apartment that he never fixed up. There were things still in boxes from his move a decade earlier. In his mind, he was waiting for the future in order to take action—a future that would never arrive.

"Consequently, our relationship was hollow. There was no opportunity to enjoy each other or to get to know one another. He stopped living in the present because he was so future oriented. As a result, I ended our relationship. He lost what was right in front of him, the future he truly wanted. If he had only been detached from the outcome he wanted so badly, we probably would have been married."

While waiting for the future to arrive, we allow the here and now to slip away, and we fail to enjoy the moment. Instead, attach yourself to the present—this very instant. This will facilitate detachment from the future. Ironically, in doing so, your desired future is more likely to materialize. This concept applies to all relationships—romantic, platonic, and business.

Let Go of the Outcome

A woman I know, Deborah, once told me about a wonderful experience she had many years ago right after college, which is a great example of reattaching yourself to something bigger and more inspirational than the traditional goal. To make a few extra dollars, she worked at a clothing store part time. Friends of hers were also working there, so she thought it would be fun.

One day the store announced a competition. They would give monetary prizes to the sales reps that sold the most clothing during the competition period. Most of the girls were quite eager and excited at the prospect of making some extra money. Besides, winning a competition is always a good ego boost.

But Deborah wasn't interested. A competition to sell more did not appeal to her. She decided to play a different game, one that did excite her. Her game was to serve the customers as well as she could. She would spend as much time with each of them as necessary. If the store did not have the best item for the customer, Deborah would recommend another store. Her purpose was to take better care of each individual. She was completely detached from selling anything, let alone winning the competition.

As the competition progressed, the other sales reps worked diligently to close the deals as quickly as possible. The number of customers served and the speed of service became critical. This was hard work for the other girls. Deborah was having fun. She took her time, got to know the customers and better understand their needs.

When the competition was over, who won? You are probably not surprised to find that Deborah won the competition by a wide margin. People like to buy from someone who is interested in serving them. She detached herself from the goal of selling and in the process became a better sales person. Think about your own personal experiences. Would you want to buy from the stereotypical used-car salesman who is playing hardball to make the sale? Or would you rather buy from someone whom you trust, respect, and believe that he has your best interests in mind?

People have a sixth sense. They can tell when you are doing something for your benefit rather than theirs. You cannot hide your feelings. Others will pick up on your subtle beliefs. If you can't hide your limits and inadequacies, you certainly cannot hide your true intentions.

Even if you are not in a sales role at work, you are in a sales role in life. You are constantly selling your ideas and concepts. It is through these sales efforts that our greatest aspirations materialize.

If you have fun and play with possibility, people will be attracted to you. They will want to help you. Besides, if you are enjoying the process, regardless of whether or not you are successful in achieving the outcome, you had fun during the journey.

Attach to the Service of Others

Not only does Deborah's story illustrate a powerful way of selling, but it also highlights a powerful way of remaining detached. A higher level of living is when you go beyond detaching from specific outcomes and you detach from yourself. In order to do this, you need to reattach yourself to something else — helping and serving others.

By attaching yourself to others, the rewards come to you. When you help yourself, you get only one reward. If you help 10 people you get 10 rewards. When you do this you are always at peace. You experience joy at a deep level.

One person who lives this way is David Wood, the Vice President of Sales for the Americas for Bose Corporation, the well-known developer of speakers and stereo systems. We met in a conference room at the new Bose sales offices in a suburb of Boston.

David feels fortunate. He has always been a bit of a music and stereo buff. Therefore, working for a company that makes such products is ideal. He started off by saying, "I don't know that I could be nearly as effective if I were selling something that I was not passionate about." David admits that he comes from a very driven family, one that has achieved quite a bit. "My father is the head of Rocketdyne, a division of Boeing, that is a primary contractor to NASA. He is very driven and achievement oriented. He has done remarkable things and has been a role model. In our family, we couldn't go through life slacking off or not investing time and energy wisely."

Early in our conversation, David said he has one overarching purpose in life: "Enabling my strengths and virtues to help others." He continued, "If I am going to invest my time and energy, these are the things I need to do. So I am continually using that as a filter for determining how to invest my time and what to focus on at home and at work."

Because this sense of purpose is so important to him, he encourages everyone in his organization to figure out what it is for them. "A lot of driven people are not happy. For me happiness is measured each and every day. How did I make a difference? I'm personally satisfied at the end of the day if I made a difference for someone personally. If someone's efforts were furthered along with my help. If some goal or output or project was accomplished. If I recognized and rewarded someone's efforts. I have this intense desire to feel like I have made an investment in someone else and the company. I am not driven by money or status. I'm not even comfortable partaking in privileged company benefits. Rather, I am driven by contribution, what I do, and the value I add."

Given his goal-free attitude, I asked him if he believes that he is more successful and satisfied than others. He admits, "That is really subjective and I can't compare myself to anyone else. However, I have achieved much more than I ever expected to achieve. I've done pretty well. Fifteen years ago I would never have thought I would be in the situation I am in." David's next lily pad? "Because I love to contribute, I think that my next move might be teaching. This is in line with my purpose of serving others."

David has been admittedly fortunate. He works for a company that makes a product he enjoys and believes in. More importantly, the culture and values of the company reflect his own personal beliefs and values. "I never felt as though I had to be someone other than who I am." I asked him what he would do if there was a major cultural change at the company leading to a misalignment between the company values and his values? Without the slightest hesitation, his answer was, "Leave." David is a perfect example of someone who lives by values and integrity. He has attached himself to the service of others. In doing so, he created a flow and lightness in his life.

Become the Flow

During my travels, there was an informal lunch organized in my honor in Montclair, New Jersey. One attendee, upon learning about my book, suggested I meet his friend Paul D'Souza, who lived in a suburb of Atlanta. Given my hectic travel schedule and exhaustion from the driving and interviews, I did not plan to follow up with Paul. Rather I intended to continue on to the next leg of the journey.

While driving down Interstate 85 from Charlotte, North Carolina to Atlanta, my cell phone rang. It was Paul. He wanted to know if I was interested in interviewing him. Honestly, I wanted to say "no." He lived nearly two hours out of my way and I was eager to get to Atlanta. But something in my head said, "Trust the process and go with the flow." So I drove to Elberton, Georgia, where I was greeted by a very cheerful man with a huge smile who extended his arm for a warm handshake. This was Paul. I instantly felt as if I had known him all my life. He felt the same way about me. I soon met his sister, brother-in-law, mother, and dogs, everyone living happily together. We sat outside on his patio, played with the dogs, listened to the birds chirp, and began our conversation. Paul is a certified energy healer who developed a philosophy called "Wha-Dho," a framework for living a life of harmony by becoming aware of your spiritual reality. He moved to the United States from India in 1987 with a Masters in Social Work. He also teaches Qi-Gong, a practice that, like Tai Chi, manipulates the body's energy. Although Paul is a highly "enlightened" and spiritual person, he surprised me with conversation about his libido, sex, beautiful women, Latin dancing, and living life fully and on the edge. For someone so connected with the universe, he is also quite grounded.

In discussing his philosophy, Paul said, "People say 'go with the flow.' But in fact going with the flow is a dichotomy. It indicates a separation of two pieces, you and the universe. It is like you are on the banks of a river and you need to jump in. The river is the flow, and it is taking you. The reality is, you are the river. Don't go with the flow, *become* the flow. Don't isolate yourself from the universe. Don't ask what you are supposed to do. Go into your silence through meditation and tap into the collective. Then you become the flow and are one with the universe. When you become the flow, you have total alignment and clarity of who you are."

Paul believes that a successful life, one of true fulfillment, cannot be benchmarked against another person's status or against religious doctrines. You are successful only if you are in sync with "what the universe wants." "The key for me," he says, "is to figure out my role, my sheet music. I don't worry about who, why, and what. I just keep in time and do my piece. I am not here to save the world or to be famous. I am here to do my part. I stand in a place in which I have such beautiful alignment that I know I am doing what I am supposed to be doing." He is detached from a life that moves in a particular direction.

"It doesn't mean that your problems disappear. It doesn't mean you will be successful financially. It doesn't mean you will marry the prettiest girl on the block. It means that when you show up for every moment you are clear about what you have to offer that moment."

Goal-free individuals not only wade in a rich river of interest, they become the river—the experience. They immerse themselves in what they do while not fighting the currents. Life is unpredictable. Goals are an attempt to control the uncontrollable. Over the years I have heard many people say that "life is hard." I believe it is only difficult for those who choose to live it that way. Life can be spectacularly simple if you go with the flow. Or better yet, become the flow.

Focus on Living

At times, detachment can be critical to survival. One woman I know works as a grief counselor, helping families who have suffered from the loss or prolonged illness of a loved one. A very difficult job indeed. She explains that people who suffer from terminal cancer or other diseases are much more likely to live if they try hard and don't give up. She asked, "Isn't giving up the same as detachment? Wouldn't that hasten someone's death?"

Absolutely not. Detachment is not about giving up hope. It is about not being attached to surviving. When you are focused on surviving, life becomes a struggle. Rather you should focus on living. When you live powerfully for today rather than worrying about surviving into the future, you have more hope and more possibility in your life.

Another person I met told me the story of a friend of hers who is living with AIDS. After her friend was first diagnosed with the disease, his health went on a rapid decline. He and his wife tried everything to help him battle the disease and fight to survive. They tried various doctors and specialists, Western medicine, Eastern medicine, herbal remedies, tests, cutting-edge drugs— whatever they could do. His focus was to do everything he could to survive.

Unfortunately, nothing worked. He kept getting worse and worse. After one particular stint in the hospital, he came home to spend what he thought might be his last days. That morning he lay down on the couch, in tremendous pain, and couldn't move all day. He decided that this was it. He was going to die. So he let go of surviving—not his will to live, but his focus on surviving. That was the turning point for him. Miraculously, he started to get better and, seven years later, he is living and living well.

Detachment is critical for Goal-Free Living. It's ultimately how we get free of our goals. It allows you to really live your life. It increases your pleasure. It helps you focus on the present. It makes you more appealing to those around you. And paradoxically, it increases the odds of your achieving your aspirations, no matter how big and bold they are.

Making It Happen

Detachment does not equate to indifference, being blasé, or doing nothing at all. Detachment actually serves as a commitment to the future while focusing on the present. Detachment is a mindset that is not always easy to achieve. Here are some thoughts, techniques, and questions to help you become or remain detached.

HAVE BIG AND BOLD ASPIRATIONS, NOT ACHIEVABLE GOALS

Goals are specific, measurable, and achievable. Having goals can set you up for failure since you can easily become discouraged by a lack of progress. As Marshall Field, the founder of the large Chicago department store chain once said, "One of the secrets of not having a nervous breakdown is not having goals." Instead of defining a goal, choose a big and bold aspiration. Something inspiring, yet potentially unattainable. If you know your aspiration is beyond your reach, then you won't feel stressed about achieving it. The future becomes a context for the present rather than a place to get to. This aids in detachment.

DON'T TRY

Trying too hard is the surest way of failing. It makes you appear desperate and untrustworthy. When you find yourself really wanting something, look in the mirror and tell yourself you don't really want it. This doesn't mean that you don't believe in yourself or your project. It only means that the outcome is the outcome, and that you are more committed to being true to yourself than you are to selling out to achieve a specific result. Remember, you are always in selling mode, selling your ideas and concepts. Rather than hard sell, have fun and play with possibility. People will be attracted to you and want to help.

THE DIFFICULTIES OF DETACHMENT

Recognize that there are some areas of your life where detachment may be quite difficult. In what areas of your life do you feel insecure, or the risks seem too high? Quite often this is due to a scarcity mentality, a belief that there is a limited supply of jobs, money, dates, or whatever. However, this scarcity is only an illusion caused by your need to have more. Rather than hurrying through life to the next milestone, stop, reflect, and enjoy where you are now. Create an abundance mentality.

DON'T STOP A BAD HABIT, REPLACE IT WITH A GOOD HABIT

It is difficult to quit any bad habit, because the brain naturally ignores the word "quit" and instead begins to crave that which you are trying to stop doing. Rather than focusing on quitting one habit, attach yourself to something more empowering. Instead of a restrictive diet that has you stop eating unhealthy foods, attach yourself to eating a certain amount of something healthy. When you focus on healthy eating, your mind is less interested in the bad stuff. And if you get a craving, allow yourself to splurge from time to time.

ATTACH TO THE SERVICE OF OTHERS

Instead of striving for more money, be a person who provides more value. This is the surest way to be successful. This is about detaching from yourself (what you want), and reattaching yourself to the service of others (what others need). Measure happiness by whether you made a difference. By doing so, you will provide greater meaning in your life, and you will be helping others in the process. In doing so, prosperity—broadly defined—is more likely to come your way.

Using the
Eight Secrets

Setting Your Compass

Just trust yourself. Then you will know how to live.
—*Johann Wolfgang von Goethe,
playwright and philosopher*

$\mathcal{T}$he book you are reading was not supposed to be. When I traveled the country in the summer of 2003, I was not looking to write about Goal-Free Living. I wasn't even thinking of writing a personal development book. My intention was to write a business book on creativity—a follow-up to my previous book, *24/7 Innovation*.

During that pivotal summer, I decided to take a working vacation. My drive across the country originated as an attempt to find inspiring places to write. I had planned to sit on the beach, sit in the mountains, and work on this book on creativity—a book based on my experiences in the corporate world.

Only five days prior to the commencement of my trip, I realized that this would be a great opportunity to meet and interview creative people—artists, entrepreneurs, inventors—to add flavor to the book and enrich it with interesting stories. So I began what I called my "Creative America Tour." However, as I conducted the interviews, I realized that the topic of creativity, although interesting, wasn't what had me fascinated with the people I met. What I found was that they lived creative lives. They lived differently from others. Instead of focusing on creativity, I began to focus on creative living.

Just like in sailing, instead of going mechanically from point A to point B, I allowed the waves and the wind to influence my course. I ended up in places I never expected to be. I met people I never intended to interview. A voodoo priest was never on my original target list (see the Some Frequently Asked Questions section for that story). As a result, the book developed into something that had little to do with my original intention.

This trip and the wonderful surprises along the way are a great metaphor for the way you can live your life. I could have developed my hypotheses about creativity, determined exactly whom I would interview, planned my trip in its entirety, and then followed those plans. I would have met the people I expected to meet. I would have gathered data to support my creativity thesis. I would have been efficient. Had I done this, and treated the trip as a goal, I am certain that I would have been successful in writing a book on corporate creativity. Maybe it would have been a great book.

Instead, I chose a different way. Rather than trying to gather data for my creativity book, I chose a less predictable path of new possibilities. Instead of efficiency, I opted for the path of adventure. In the end, what emerged was something far beyond my wildest expectations. I could never have conceived the Goal-Free Living concept before the trip. It had to unfold naturally as part of my exploration.

Traveling 12,000 miles and meeting 150 people was an extraordinary experience. It provided me with many new perspectives on life, some of which reinforced what I had instinctively be-lieved to be true. It also convinced me that there is no right or wrong way to live your life. Everyone has a unique personality, and your personality type can determine your preferred mode of operation. Maybe you are someone who truly likes plans and goals because they keep you focused and provide a level of pre-dictability. Maybe you get great pleasure from a beautiful house and luxury cars. Maybe you prefer security and comfort over ad-venture and spontaneity. If the way you live your life truly works for you, then stick to it. But if you feel as though something is missing, that there could be more to life, that you want more pas-sion, then consider trying something new, even if at first it feels uncomfortable or unnatural.

Setting Sail

Goals provide comfort and predictability. They make us more ef-ficient. But in life, you can't plan out passion. The best experi-ences unfold naturally. Treat life as an exploration. Rather than speeding toward your destination, enjoy the adventure. The best paths are the ones we know nothing about and would never have visited unless we allowed ourselves to meander.

Think of your life as a blank sheet of paper. Eliminate the "shoulds" and "musts" you have let dictate your life. Instead, focus on your aspirations and dreams. Create an expansive life full of possibility. Only by changing the way you see the world can you truly change your actions. Don't worry about how to execute these eight secrets. Just try them. Play with them in small doses. Practice the ones that feel right. Try on one at a time, one day at a time. Over time, you will begin to live them effortlessly and without thinking. As the stories in this book demonstrate, these eight secrets will help you create an extraordinary life.

I look forward to hearing about your own personal battles with goals and the wonderful successes that emerge.

Go to www.GoalFree.com for discussion forums on a variety of topics relating to Goal-Free Living. There is even a place where you can contribute your own goal-free experiences. Feel free to contact me any time via e-mail at Steve@GoalFree.com.

One Person's Transformation from Goalaholic to Goal-Free

$\mathcal{S}$omeone I know has, over the course of several years, had a personal transformation from a serious goalaholic to a passion-filled, goal-free individual. This epilogue is her story, in her own words.

It took me 36 years, but I finally did it. I took the plunge into married life, a life I wasn't sure would ever be. My delay toward nuptial bliss wasn't a result of many long cold nights alone. On the contrary. My husband gains much pleasure telling friends my move halfway across the country was a response to having no one left to date on the East Coast. Let's just say I was picky. I had this vision of marriage built on a foundation of movie romances and sappy novels where two individuals were cosmically bound and lived happily ever after. It was a goal that I had since childhood and was unwilling to surrender. I heard of people who had settled, and frankly, that wasn't going to be me.

I always knew what I wanted and went after it. Take my career. I knew that someday I would become an executive within a major corporation. I would be the envy of all my friends, living in a mansion, driving fancy cars, throwing lavish parties and owning homes throughout the world. I worked more hours than any of my colleagues, and was rewarded with rapid career advancement and handsome salary increases.

But my career never got in the way of my quest for love. My dating schedule matched my work schedule hour for hour. It didn't matter that I only got a mere two hours of sleep each night. I had two key goals and nothing was going to stop me!

I met guys in many of the common places: bars, on the Internet, through friends, and parties. I took up weight lifting and joined a gym in the hopes of getting men to provide me with a spot. I became a sports fanatic so that I could mingle with men and talk their language. I even hung out in stogy bars puffing rings of smoke with my male counterparts despite how disgusting it tasted and how horrible it made me feel. I was going to find my guy no matter what it took.

And what would this guy be like? He had to be tall and of course muscular so I could melt into his arms as he protected me from the perils of the world. Not looks alone, he would be well educated and well traveled. He would take me to exotic places, speaking the language wherever we went.

And family. Family was always important to me. Growing up, my parents supported my every interest. They attended every football game as I clumsily marched in the band. They stayed up to help me study so that I could graduate tops in my class. They went to every musical, beaming as though they were watching their baby on Broadway. Having been blessed with a family that positively influenced my life, it was imperative that my man have a wonderful family as well.

When I met my now husband, he was just a guy, a target, a possibility. But, he did not in any way fit the picture that I had created for myself. His red hair and freckles made him a first for me. His high school education, unseemly past, and disjointed family also did not fit my mold. I didn't really think that I would end up with him. He did not evoke that "toe curl" feeling I so passionately pursued. That feeling that rips through your body as you gaze into each other's eyes. That uncontrollable yearning that leaves you breathless and a bit faint. Like in the movies.

Nonetheless, I made a 1,200 mile move.

To be completely honest, I think I used this as an excuse to leave my job. While contrary to my goals of status and wealth, I was finding my job stifling. The closer I was to attaining my goal, the unhappier I became. I chose not to analyze this too deeply and simply took the jump. It was a calculated jump, mind you, as I wouldn't make the move until I had secured a comparable job with commensurate pay.

A conflict developed within me. How could I relocate for a person who did not provide me with the movie version of love? Was I settling? No. I determined that if the relationship should fail, I was still on my career path.

The day he asked me to marry him, I did all I could not to cry. These were not tears of joy, but tears of anguish and conflict. On one hand, I was with a gentleman that made me feel a way I had never felt before. For the first time, I felt a calmness, a completeness, a wholeness. But on the other hand, he had red hair. Instead of higher education he chose the military. Let me be clear: I have the highest regard for the dedicated men and women who serve our country. The real problem was that "chose" might be a misleading term in this statement. In his case, the military was chosen for him in lieu of many long nights in a different hell—behind bars.

And his family. While each member of his family was wonderful, they were not a family. There were no big Thanksgiving celebrations. No family reunions. No group vacations. No childhood memories to laugh about. There was an ex-wife, actually two, his adopted daughter of 11, his mother, the father who adopted him, his birth grandmother, a sister, and a myriad of foster families.

I couldn't walk away. And I couldn't stay. My quest for my perfect man was etched indelibly into my mind. But was this ideal really what I had wanted? I wondered if I could even discern what I wanted from what I thought other people felt I should have. Not just when it came to my selection of men, but in every facet of my life.

The clothing I wore, the car I drove, the houses I lived in, the hairstyle I donned, the body I sculpted, the career goals I chose, the college I attended, the men I courted. These were all things that I thought would gain me recognition and approval from my peers, my family, and my friends. But I couldn't identify what about these things even appealed to me. The truth was that I had designed my life and calculated my every move based on a set of principles that I had read about in magazines, seen on the silver screen, or learned in school. But after 34 years, how does one break the cycle?

I struggled to identify why I felt so empty. While I had amassed all of the material and aesthetic goals I had set out to achieve, I still felt as though there was something missing. What did I want to do with my life? Where was I going? Who was I?

It simply became a matter of choosing. The fence on which I had been sitting was becoming increasingly uncomfortable and I had to jump. I just had to choose. So I chose marriage. Why, I don't know. I veered from the path that I so ferociously sought. Away from the image of my knight in shining armor with whom I would ride off into the sunset.

But a curious thing happened. Once I chose, my world shifted. Opportunities presented themselves that I had never seen before. A life filled with quiet nights of gentle cuddling on the couch. A life of stability and splendor. A life built upon years of knowing that the person that I have chosen has chosen me back. A life based on familiarity and cohesion.

I developed wonderful friendships with women who, in my single life, were no more than props used for meeting men. I was able to build a relationship with an individual who knew me, the real me. And he loved me, wrinkles and all.

His education, while an initial deterrent in my original scheme, melted away as I saw that his wisdom and talent, his drive and ambition, and his innate intelligence far exceeded those of more scholarly types. His family, by conventional standards, was shattered and broken, peppered with ex-wives, estranged family members, and strife. But that was not at all the case. We created a network of loved ones even more spectacular than the traditional family that I had grown accustomed to. We spend holidays with his ex. We have folded my family into hers, blurring the boundaries of what most would call family. We have ignited a unique relationship that seems unfathomable to most.

What had happened? I abandoned my goal. My vision, well, society's vision of the perfect relationship. I have built something different. I didn't settle. I simply recreated a different world, an unplanned world. And for that I owe my life!

Becoming Goal Free

I suspect by now, it is apparent that I had not been goal-free for most of my adult years. But I had taken my first step, and it was a doozie. And now that I have had a taste of what it feels like to let go of a goal, one would surmise that it would be easy to apply this valuable practice throughout all other aspects of my life. Unfortunately, not so.

While my marriage filled one void, it left another—time. I no longer needed to expend countless hours seeking out my true love. So now what? Up to this point, I hadn't cultivated a sense of self. All my activities centered on those that would find me a man. I was beginning to realize that my chosen pastimes, especially smoking cigars, were not enjoyable to me. I decided to invest this extra time into achieving my other goal, my career.

For the next four years I worked tirelessly, painstakingly and without fail. No lunches, no breaks. Pure commitment and dedication through and through.

I worked 10, 12, 15 hours a day. These mounted onto my already insurmountable three-hour commute. I became increasingly agitated. I was slowly slipping into a place where I was seldom able to sleep, disinterested in having anything to eat, and my sex life took a nose dive. I was too tired to do much of anything with the exception of wearily kissing my husband on the cheek on my way home from work on my way up to bed.

The more agitated I became, the less I was able to focus on my work. So, I worked that much longer. And the vicious cycle continued. It was reminiscent of a few years back when I ended up taking a leave of absence due to extreme burnout. I had 102 temperature, a severe bronchial cough, and could barely keep my eyes open. My boss pulled me aside. Her words still stay with me today.

She said in a low but stern voice, "I am concerned about your performance."

My performance?, I thought. Wasn't I her model employee, working long hours, overachieving, and exceeding all the goals set forth by this manager?

"I have to question your judgment. And in this job, judgment is critical."

I was still perplexed. My judgment? Wasn't I the one who had resolved some of the most complex situations that came through our department? Wasn't I the employee with the countless accolades displayed in my office?

She continued. "If you choose to come into work while

being this sick, I have to question your judgment. It is just plain stupid."

With that, she sent me home to think. She shattered my reality. I was living under the premise that only the most dedicated employees go to work despite any adversity in their life. I had a set of rules. Where this premise came from, I still to this day do not know. But it was then that I knew I had lost all control.

As an adult, I should have learned from my mistakes. Even with this past experience, I found myself repeating history. Why was this happening? It hadn't always been this way. I remember when I first started out in my career, I was always so blissful. I was passionate about my work and loved the interaction, the relationships, and the gratification I received knowing that I was able to make a difference in my customers' lives.

But as I came closer to achieving my goal, a fancy title and a six-figure income, something changed. I was becoming increasingly dissatisfied. I had always worked long hours for as long as I could remember. But the hours were never a problem until recently. Perhaps it was the fact that I wasn't doing what I loved anymore. The further I ascended up the corporate ladder the further away I was getting from the activities I had loved. But how could I go back? I was committed. I have come so far. I couldn't quit now! Or could I?

There was a two-week stretch where I remember things getting increasingly worse. I cried virtually every night on my way home from work and my husband and I were fighting continually over the late hours I was keeping and my lack of responsiveness. I hadn't slept in weeks.

One night, in the grocery store, I was reaching into the poultry freezer when a blood pressure machine in the pharmaceutical section caught my eye. I decided to slip the cuff on and give it a whirl. I watched the numbers flicker within the two boxes marked "diastolic" and "systolic." Apparently I was an overachiever even in my blood pressure. Perhaps it was a fluke. But each night, when I returned to the grocery store to pick up the evening's dinner, the numbers on the monitor continued to creep up. My husband urged me to go to the local clinic, which stayed open late at night.

The doctor explained that I needed to check myself in at the emergency room down the street. My blood pressure was critical and I needed to tend to it immediately. As I lay in the emergency room with the EKG monitor hooked to my chest, there was this overwhelming sense of relief. I realized that I had once again stepped onto a treadmill, this time a career track, and I wanted to get off. My health would give me a convenient excuse for once again bowing out gracefully from my stifling job. The very next day, I stepped down from the position I fought so hard for. I felt I could save face with a reason such as my health. Instead of appearing as a quitter, I was showered with concern and understanding.

I look back on that day, furious that I needed an excuse. I was miserable. Isn't that excuse enough?

I didn't understand it at the time, but this situation proved to be a significant turning point in my life. I began working from home, giving me back a minimum of three hours in commuting time alone. I reduced my salary, relinquished my staff, and cut out all of those duties that I had hated so much! And wouldn't ya know, I became more productive in fewer hours. I received more accolades in my new role within four months than I had received in the preceding 15 years. But more importantly, I was happy. Go figure! Half my pay, a silly title that was created for my makeshift job, and I was happy. It felt like the shackles of life had been removed and I could breathe again.

It was beginning to dawn on me that the path I had paved for achieving my goals, which I know would have gotten me there, was so narrow that it left no room for much of anything else, let alone happiness. It was only when I stepped off those paths that I really began to live and it was effortless. And I wanted more!

I guess being goal free isn't necessarily a natural thing, at least not in our society. It goes counter to everything that we have been taught. And despite the wonderful results I had reached each time I was "forced" to relinquish my goals, I have often found myself wandering back to that familiar place of goal setting. Funny how it takes work to be effortless.

Appendixes

Some Frequently Asked Questions

*A*fter reading about the eight secrets, people often have lingering questions. Some of the most frequently asked ones are answered on the following pages. More information can be found on my website, www.GoalFree.com.

Is Goal-Free Living the Right Way to Live?

No. Goal-Free Living is not the right way to live. The eight secrets are only distinctions, and distinctions are not the truth. Rather they are like the lessons taught in a wine-tasting class I took many years ago. Prior to these lessons, all wine tasted pretty much the same to me. A fine Bordeaux would be somewhat indistinguishable from a less expensive bottle. But after wine tasting, I had new distinctions, such as legs, nose (bouquet), and finish. Now a great wine tastes incredible. Conversely, wines of lesser quality don't interest me as much—and I know why. When you have distinctions, great experiences are even greater, and mediocre experiences become only tolerable. Goal-Free Living and its secrets are distinctions for life. They make us aware of our passions and have us gravitate toward more enjoyable paths through life.

Distinctions aren't real or the truth. They just provide different ways of looking at the world to help us better understand and appreciate things around us, whether they are wines or life. Just as wine experts each prefer different styles and variety of wines, each of us has a preferred way of living our life.

Can You Have Goals in a Life of Goal-Free Living?

Absolutely. Goal-Free Living is being free from the burden of goals, not free from goals in their entirety. Sometimes goals are useful for getting things done in life. Unfortunately for many, their goals have a grip on them in a way that prevents them from having a free-flowing, passionate life. They are goalaholics. The relationship between goals and goalaholism can be viewed as similar to the relationship between alcohol and alcoholism. Alcohol itself is not bad. In fact, many studies suggest that alcohol in moderation, in particular red wine (the *right* kind of alcohol), can be beneficial to your health. However, when too much alcohol is consumed, the impact can be detrimental.

Goals are similar. When you use the right kind of goals (*healthy* goals, or as I prefer to call them, "paths") in moderation, they may help you achieve specific objectives you desire in your life. Focus can be beneficial in getting things done. Since we live in a goal-oriented society, even the most goal-free person has goals thrust upon him. My publisher has given me deadlines and guidelines for this book. In order to avoid the wrath of my editor, the completion of the book on time has become a goal. And we'd all better have a goal of paying our taxes by April 15th if we want to avoid penalties from the Internal Revenue Service. How you relate to your goals (detachment, appreciation, living in the moment) is what differentiates healthy goals from unhealthy goals.

Certainly Some People Need More Goals, Don't They?

True. Some people would benefit from more goals. While walking along the streets of New York City, I was watching some homeless youths on a park bench. Surely, I thought, goals for these individuals would be valuable. Even small goals to get them moving in the direction of a better life. I then glanced up into the windows of the office buildings above and saw suited business people running around frantically. The stress was obvious even from where I stood on the street corner. These people would benefit from fewer goals. Less rigid goals. That is the paradox of goals. You need goals first, before you can ditch them. When you are starting out and have nothing—including motivation—anything you do to further develop yourself—even the smallest goal—is a step in the right direction. The problem is, for many people, after relying on goals for a while they become a crutch. If you learn that goals can help you achieve a predictable result, you tend to rely on them for this comfort—a safety net.

I am reminded of a cooking class I took many years ago. First we were taught the principles of cooking. Beginners, like me, learned how to boil water. As we progressed, we got more advanced and learned about different cooking techniques (baking, broiling, and sautéing). We then learned about different spices, and which spices are used in which dishes. The lessons about principles continued for the first few classes, until we were ready to start preparing a meal. At this point we began to rely on recipes to help us prepare our dishes. Recipes tell you the exact amount of each ingredient, the exact temperatures at which to cook, and the exact order in which to do things. With the help of cookbooks we were able to make many great meals, with predictable and repeatable results. Goals are life's cookbook—recipes for predictable results. This can be very handy, but it also can be limiting. It reduces your ability to improvise, to be creative, and to try new things. That is why the best cooks, after using recipes during their training, progress from the safety of the cookbook and back to the principles. They begin to ad-lib. They no longer rely on a specific formula. A good chef could probably only have become so by using recipes in the beginning. But to truly excel, he needs to have the confidence to be creative, go beyond the cookbook, and try new things. Being goal-free is a chance for you to ditch the recipe and improvise in your life.

Is This Approach Right for Everybody? Are There People Who Are Happy with a Goal-Oriented Life?

The goal-free lifestyle will resonate with some people, but certainly not with everyone. There are some people who truly prefer a goal-oriented lifestyle. Your preferred mode of operation will largely depend on your personality type. One of the most popular personality tests is the Myers-Briggs Type Indicator (MBTI), which has four categories of preferences. The category which most likely determines your propensity for goals is your "life management" orientation—judging versus perceiving.

People who are most likely to be goal-oriented are what the MBTI calls the "judgers." As a rule, judgers like to plan their work and work the plans. They have a preference for a structured and organized life. Common words to describe their view of life include: plan, decide, structure, organize, firmness, and control.

On the other end of the spectrum are the "perceivers." They tend to operate from a more "seat of the pants" perspective. They prefer a more spontaneous and flexible lifestyle. Words they like are: open, flow, adapt, explore, meander, inquire, flexibility, and spontaneous.

In our modern goal-oriented society, we are led to believe that the judgers are king. Sometimes this forces perceivers to emulate the goal-oriented lifestyle, even though it is not appropriate for them. The opportunity is to recognize that there are different ways of living. Perceivers should be proud of having a goal-free existence. It is their natural mode of operating. Judgers might learn from the perceivers how to loosen up and go with the flow. The great thing about the MBTI is that there is no "right" personality type. MBTI is about our natural preferences. All Myers-Briggs types are appropriate at different times and situations. Find what works best for you, while remaining open to new concepts.

Will I Get Results Right Away?

Yes. The changes associated with Goal-Free Living are partly attitudinal shifts. By "wanting what you have," you will instantly have a greater level of satisfaction in your life. By "remaining detached" you will reduce the stress in your life. Some of the shifts are behavioral in nature. "Seeking out adventure" means trying new things, no matter how small, in order to gain new experiences. "Becoming a people magnet" is about meeting new people who can enrich your experience of life. Most importantly, the goal-free approach is about focusing on the present, enjoying where you are now rather than focusing on the future. It really is about "How to have the life you want NOW!"

How Can I Possibly Be Successful without Goals?

Although goals may be a way of achieving success, sometimes focusing on the present can bring even greater rewards.

In 2004, the New England Patriots football team broke all records for the longest winning streak in National Football League history: 21 games in a row. This is an amazing accomplishment, especially in today's environment of free agents. During a press conference after the twentieth consecutive win, Head Coach Bill Belichick was asked to comment about their string of victories. He replied, "We did not have a 20-game winning streak. We had 20 *one-game* winning streaks." His philosophy was to play each game the best they could. They did not worry about the past; although they can learn from it, they can't change what has already happened. And they never looked to the future. Worrying about where you are going means you take your sights off the ball. If the players do their best on each play of each game, then that is all they can do.

What if you played life looking for 30,000 one-day winning streaks? That means each day is the best you can make it. You won't win every game, and every day is not going to be perfect. However, with this attitude, you can't lose in the long run. In fact, you may just break some success records of your own.

What Are Common Misconceptions about Goal-Free Living?

Goal-Free Living conjures up images in peoples' minds. Let me dispel some common misconceptions about goal-free people. Goal-free people are *not*:

- Irresponsible and selfish. People who are goal-free do not just throw away everything they have worked for. They don't even necessarily change jobs. In fact, they are very responsible individuals. While living without the burden of traditional goals, people can be more responsible to themselves, their family, and society. They are motivated for the right reasons (as defined by themselves) rather than by just money or status. They find ways of creating passion in their current circumstances, and only make changes when they truly make sense. Goal-Free Living is not about abdication; it is not an excuse for not being successful.

- Lazy and narcissistic. Goal-Free Living is certainly not about sitting on your butt all day watching Jerry Springer and eating bonbons. Pursuing aspirations that drive passion is very different from the pursuit of simple hedonistic pleasures. Being goal-free does not imply that you should become a ski bum simply because you enjoy skiing as a hobby. Goal-Free Living is about finding something with real meaning in your life, playing hard, having fun, being responsible, and being in action. If skiing is your true passion and you can find a way of making it work in your life, then skiing may be a good path for you. Goal-Free Living is about active participation in the things that matter most to you.

- Directionless. Being goal-free does not mean living without direction. It is not about abandoning your worldly goods and becoming a nomad. It is not existential despair. People who are goal-free have a clear sense of direction as dictated by their internal compass and their aspiration. Goal-free individuals move forward with conviction and intention, but not attachment. They are driven by passion and intuition rather than ego and plans. Discover your passions and play full out.

I Read about a Yale Study That Showed That the Most Successful People Set Clear Goals. Doesn't This Run Counter to Goal-Free Living?

I get asked this question quite often, as this study has been cited numerous times by authors and motivational speakers. The story, as told by many, goes like this: In 1953, researchers surveyed Yale University's graduating seniors to determine how many of them had specific, written goals for their future. The answer: 3 percent. Twenty years later, researchers polled the surviving members of the Class of 1953—and found that the 3 percent with goals had accumulated more personal financial wealth than the other 97 percent of the class combined! There are two problems with this story. First, just because these people attained wealth does not imply they attained happiness. Success and satisfaction are not the same thing. But more importantly, this widely told story is an urban legend. *Fast Company* magazine debunked this myth back in 1997. No such study was done. The magazine noted that people like Forrest Mars Jr., now chairman and CEO of Mars, Inc., listed "no" for employment possibilities back at Yale. (*Fast Company*: "If Your Goal Is Success, Don't Consult These Gurus": Dec 1996/Jan 1997.)

Who Is the Most Interesting Person You Met during Your Travels?

This question is impossible to answer. There were so many incredible and fascinating people. Certainly one of the more *unusual* people was John T. Martin, a Voodoo priest in New Orleans who is also the curator of the Voodoo museum there. During our dinner together in the French Quarter, he told me that just by touching someone, he can foresee his or her death (I avoided contact with him; I want to keep my death plans a secret, especially from myself!). He proceeded to tell me the story of a man from Jacksonville, Florida, who came to him just two days prior for a reading. John T. (as he is known) touched the man's arm and immediately asked if he had diabetes and heart disease. He did. John T. then told him that he had only two years to live, and that could not be changed. However, the path toward his death could be altered. He told the man that if he did not change the way he lived, within a year his health would fail and his last year on this earth would be a living hell. However, if he made radical changes to his diet, exercise, and lifestyle, he would live a peaceful and enjoyable two years. Whether you believe in John T's abilities or not, there is an interesting lesson here. In our goal-oriented society, we are often too focused on where we are going. We pay too little attention to where we are today and how to maximize the pleasure we get from daily life. John T. showed the way to his man from Florida. What if our only destiny (or final destination) is death? Even without the voodoo, it's worth asking yourself what you can do today to live a more passionate and creative life.

Take the "Are You a Goalaholic?" Quiz

To take the quiz, for each statement, please select the one option that best applies:

1. I am in awe of how fulfilling my life is.

   Strongly Agree   Agree   Neutral   Disagree   Strongly Disagree

2. Despite my success, I often feel as though something is missing from my life.

   Agree   Tend to Agree   Neutral   Tend to Disagree   Disagree

3. I sometimes get the feeling that I am living my life in a way that satisfies others (friends, family, co-workers) more than it satisfies me.

   Agree   Tend to Agree   Neutral   Tend to Disagree   Disagree

4. Once I have set a goal, I will stay committed to achieving it even if my interests have changed.

   Agree   Tend to Agree   Neutral   Tend to Disagree   Disagree

5. I find myself saying that "I will be happy when . . ." (fill in the blank).

   Agree   Tend to Agree   Neutral   Tend to Disagree   Disagree

6. I am focused on, and living for, something I want in the future.

Agree   Tend to Agree   Neutral   Tend to Disagree   Disagree

7. I am good about creating clear plan(s) for achieving my goal(s).

Agree   Tend to Agree   Neutral   Tend to Disagree   Disagree

8. I get disappointed when I am unsuccessful in achieving the results I pursue.

Agree   Tend to Agree   Neutral   Tend to Disagree   Disagree

9. I am willing to sacrifice today for the future.

Agree   Tend to Agree   Neutral   Tend to Disagree   Disagree

10. I encourage those that I care about to pursue goals that I think are best for them.

Agree   Tend to Agree   Neutral   Tend to Disagree   Disagree

Go to Appendix C to score your results.

Score the "Are You a Goalaholic?" Quiz

Question #1
(non-scoring question)

If you answered "strongly agree," then clearly you are living a life that works for you. Even if you are goal-oriented, don't change a thing. In fact, if you are interested in sharing the story of your life with us, we may include your story on our web site. Congratulations! You don't need to score your results.

If you answered "agree," then you are better than average. Regardless, many people have convinced themselves they are happier than they really are because they don't know what is possible. Consider that maybe your rating is somewhat inflated and that there is even more room for improvement. Loosening the grip that goals have on your life may help you have a happier life. Continue scoring your results.

If you answered anything else (i.e., neutral, disagree, or strongly disagree), then consider the possibility that goals are the reason why your life is not miraculous. To really determine if they are the culprit, continue scoring.

Questions #2 – #10

Give yourself the following points for each question answered:

Agree = 10, Tend to Agree = 7, Neutral = 5, Tend to Disagree = 3, Disagree = 0

Find Your Score Range to Get Your Results

55–90 POINTS: GOALAHOLIC

Perhaps it is time to check yourself into rehab! Goals have a stranglehold on your life. You have elected to put your happiness on hold for the promise of a better tomorrow, but you often find that tomorrow never comes. Or, if it does, you are left with the empty realization that "this is not *it*." While your focus and determination may have made you successful, they are also the very things that have kept you from truly leading a passion-filled and miraculous life. Wondrous opportunities may have surfaced, but your determination to see your goals through to fruition made you blind to them—or worse, had you consciously bypass them. How many of these goals were important to you at one time and, although your interests have changed, your goals did not? More than likely, you have succumbed to traditional measures of success thrust upon you by family, friends, the media, or the "Joneses." You have stopped thinking and living your own life and have allowed others to dictate it to you. You have chosen success over happiness, tomorrow over today, mediocrity over miraculous.

30–54 POINTS: BORDERLINE

It isn't too late for you. While your goals have given you direction and you haven't let them totally dominate your life, there is room for significantly more passion. It may be worth your while to do a bit of spring cleaning and toss out those goals that no longer bring you joy and passion today! Do not let yourself get too embroiled in one particular avenue (e.g., buying a house, obtaining a specific job, getting a promotion). Instead, create many options for your future, diminishing the inevitable frustration and disappointment that come from placing all of your eggs in one basket. Try new things, explore new interests, and meet new people. While you may be tempted to take on goals that appease others, do not do this at the expense of your own happiness. Be careful not to impose your goals on those around you, especially those you love, since you are particularly susceptible to thinking that you are "only doing what is best for them."

15–29 POINTS: GOAL-FREE

Ah, you are living the good life. You have truly discovered the secrets to living freely, unencumbered by the madness around you. You have taken control of your destiny in a way that others cannot even dream of. You wake up each morning embracing the miracle that is your life. More than likely you are envied by others, or perhaps even misunderstood for your sometimes unconventional approaches. But you are steadfast in ensuring that you live the life you were meant to live . . . passion-filled and miraculous.

0–14 POINTS: DIRECTIONLESS

Are you really being honest? Even the most goal-free person has some goals. Goals are often imposed upon us because, let's face it, we live in a goal-oriented society. Having some goals is okay, as long as they don't dominate your life and prevent you from being completely fulfilled. Don't confuse being goal-free with narcissism or laziness. Partying all the time, or sitting on your butt eating bonbons and watching TV, are not what Goal-Free Living is about. Goal-Free Living is experiential living. It is about being in the moment and living for today, about playing fully and passionately.

The "Are You a Goalaholic?" Online Survey Results

Highlights

- 52 percent of respondents are dissatisfied with their lives. Only 48 percent agree or strongly agree that they are in awe of how incredible their lives are.
- 76 percent agree or strongly agree that despite their success, they feel that something is missing from their lives.
- 53 percent feel that they are living their lives in a way that satisfies others more than themselves.
- 74 percent of respondents are disappointed when they are unsuccessful in achieving their goals.
- 58 percent are willing to sacrifice today for the future. An even larger percentage of respondents are focused on and living for something that they want in the future.

Detailed Results

1. I am in awe of how incredible my life is.

Strongly Agree	Agree	Neutral	Disagree	Strongly Disagree
16%	32%	26%	20%	6%

2. Despite my success, I often feel as though something is missing from my life.

Strongly Agree	Agree	Neutral	Disagree	Strongly Disagree
25%	51%	12%	9%	3%

3. I sometimes get the feeling that I am living my life in a way that satisfies others (friends, family, co-workers) more than it satisfies me.

Strongly Agree	Agree	Neutral	Disagree	Strongly Disagree
15%	38%	17%	21%	9%

4. Once I have set a goal, I will stay committed to achieving it even if my interests have changed.

Strongly Agree	Agree	Neutral	Disagree	Strongly Disagree
8%	20%	19%	41%	12%

5. I find myself saying that "I will be happy when . . ." (fill in the blank).

Strongly Agree	Agree	Neutral	Disagree	Strongly Disagree
21%	40%	15%	18%	6%

6. I am focused on, and living for, something I want in the future.

Strongly Agree	Agree	Neutral	Disagree	Strongly Disagree
21%	41%	19%	15%	4%

7. I am good about creating clear plan(s) for achieving my goal(s).

Strongly Agree	Agree	Neutral	Disagree	Strongly Disagree
11%	33%	21%	26%	9%

8. I get disappointed when I am unsuccessful in achieving the results I pursue.

Strongly Agree	Agree	Neutral	Disagree	Strongly Disagree
23%	51%	15%	9%	2%

9. I am willing to sacrifice today for the future.

Strongly Agree	Agree	Neutral	Disagree	Strongly Disagree
17%	41%	20%	17%	5%

10. I encourage those that I care about to pursue goals that I think are best for them.

Strongly Agree	Agree	Neutral	Disagree	Strongly Disagree
17%	46%	18%	14%	5%

NOTES

- The online sample size was 1,310 respondents. This is not considered to be statistically valid as it is not a random survey of the general public. Answers are only from visitors to the goalfree.com web site.
- The rating system that was used for the online survey (strongly agree, agree, neutral, disagree, strongly disagree) was changed slightly for this book (Appendix B). We discovered that most people do not pick "strongly" agree or disagree as they tend not to think in these extreme terms. The new rating system (agree, tend to agree, neutral, tend to disagree, disagree) encourages greater use of all five categories. We expect that as we gather new data, people will appear to be even more goal-oriented.

INDEX

ABOUT THE AUTHOR

*S*tephen Shapiro's successful career is based on the core belief that every individual and organization has yet to realize its full, extraordinary potential. Guided by this principle, he teaches clients how to identify and leverage their strengths, root out and overcome their weaknesses and ultimately capitalize on opportunities they never knew existed. Shapiro's career began with the international consulting firm *Accenture* where he was a leader of the firm's reengineering practice. In 1996, he established *Accenture's* Global Process Excellence Practice, and became the founder and director of the Center for Process Excellence, an R&D group focused on process, performance improvement, simulation, and innovation. In 1999 he moved to London to head the European Process Excellence Practice. In 2001, Shapiro changed direction and left the management consulting world to promote his first book, *24/7 Innovation: A Blueprint for Surviving and Thriving in an Age of Change* (McGraw-Hill). At that time he launched The 24/7 Innovation Group, a management education and research organization concentrating on innovation and break-through thinking.

In 2003, Shapiro applied the effective innovation and creativity strategy he'd developed for his clients to find even more opportunity. That summer, he set out and drove 12,000 miles around the United States and interviewed 150 people to research and write his next book, *Goal-Free Living: How to Have the Life You Want NOW!* (Wiley). In addition to writing *24/7 Innovation*, he has been a contributor to several *Economist* Intelligence Unit reports and to Bill Gates' book *Business @ the Speed of Thought*. He has also written dozens of articles published in national newspapers and magazines, including contributions to *Investor's Business Daily*, the *New York Times*, and *O, The Oprah Magazine*.

During his career, Shapiro has advised leading organizations around the world including Staples, General Electric, Lockheed Martin, ABB, Xerox, Avaya, Vodafone, BMW WilliamsF1, Frito Lay, Barclays, the Singapore government, UPS, and Bristol-Myers Squibb. He is also a frequent speaker at industry conferences including The Marketing Forum, The Forrester CIO Forum, and the Human Resources Council. He is a member of the National Speakers Association and has inspired hundreds of thousands of people in 27 countries. When he is not motivating audiences around the world, he enjoys scuba diving, wine tasting, and playing the tenor saxophone.